NUFF SED

G. P. E. SPIERS

Grosvenor House
Publishing Limited

This book is published by
Grosvenor House Publishing Ltd
Link House
140 The Broadway, Tolworth, Surrey, KT6 7HT.
www.grosvenorhousepublishing.co.uk

A CIP record for this book
is available from the British Library

ISBN 978-1-80381-656-2

Preface

This is a fictionalised history of three families who were joined in marriage and circumstances. The lives of three men, their wives, and their descendants. It tells of the children they raised and the children they lost. From Frederick Thomas Horsfall, already a third-generation lighterman, born into the poverty of East London's docklands in 1851, to his death four thousand miles and eighty-five years later in St Louis, and everything in between. They travelled the world with the royal and merchant navies; some were labourers in the midlands who emigrated to Australia, and others dock workers from London who moved to America. The family fought and died in the First World War and suffered the effects long after. The book retells acts of great kindness, acts of corruption and bullying, but more than anything, it retells the lives of an ordinary family living in extraordinary times.

The story was made possible by the amazing memories of the "East Ham Folk", Fred, Dolly, Ivy and Harry Spiers, and the collection of documents, letters, and photos my great-aunts Dolly and Ivy kept safe for over a century. The idea formulated in my mind twenty-five years ago while I was taking an eighty-year-old Dolly on one of her regular visits across the river Thames on the Woolwich Ferry to visit her sister Ivy. She related stories of her past, stories she had been told by her parents of their past and their parents' life stories. She told me of houses and areas they had lived in as we drove through London's ever-changing docklands and of the local characters she remembered. This continued as we travelled back and forth regularly over the next few years, and each new story was accompanied by the documents, faded photographs and letters she and her mother had archived in chests and boxes in the bottom of the wardrobe. Ivy then joined in with her memories on the car journeys from her home of sixty years in Plumstead, when she visited her family home In Wolsey Ave in East Ham, also back and forth on the Woolwich Ferry. She too had kept an incredible collection of letters and photos from her past.

Most other families I know have kept a few photos and an odd letter; mine have passed on primary evidence of mortgages, funeral invoices, employment, and union details. Photographs of every wedding, romance, holiday, birth and even death that occurred over the past hundred years and every other minutia of their everyday lives, without which this book would be pure guesswork. I have dramatized some liaisons and dialogues in line with the characters my great-aunts knew, most of whom they had first-hand knowledge of. Any insult this book may cause is purely unintentional on my part. "The East Ham Folk" were the kindest, most generous people I ever had the pleasure to know, and I genuinely believe if they had a bad word to say about someone, that person deserved it.

Acknowledgements

The inspiration for this book is Edie, Ivy, and Jaxon. My adorable grandchildren, who I hope someday will be proud of their ancestors who helped shape the amazing characters they are. They are also the ones we tell, 'You can do anything you want in life,' so I felt I had no excuse not to fulfil my own ambition and write this. I must mention Rebecca Lane, without whom this book would still have been written, albeit illegibly. Her patience in the face of abject ignorance can only be admired. Rebecca's editorial advice was invaluable. And last but never least, to Jo, my long-suffering wife who has had to endure years of family research. Patiently nodding when I woke her in the middle of the night when I discovered another snippet of family history that seemed so important at the time. Although, in hindsight, much of it not important enough to include in this story anyhow. Years of hearing, 'One day I am going to put it all in a book.' Well, not anymore. Until I chase another dream.

Principal Characters and Their Siblings

FREDERICK THOMAS HORSFALL (B.1851)—CHARLOTTE DOBSON (B.1848) | **RICHARD SPIRES (B.1824)—JANE SATCHELL (B.1833)** | **WILLIAM JENNINGS (B.1828)—DIANNA BROWN (B.1832)**

FLORENCE HORSFALL (B.1875)	ARTHUR WILLIAM SPIRES (B.1868)	ERNEST JENNINGS (B.1875)——ANNIE FLEWIN (B.1876)	
Charlotte Elizabeth (B.1873)	James (B.1850)	William (B.1853)	Elizabeth Jessie (B.1870)
Frederick Thomas (B.1877)	John (B.1852)	Charles (B.1855)	John (B.1873)
Rose (B.1879)	Elizabeth (B.1854)	Alfred (B.1857)	George (B.1877)
Margaret (B.1881)	Tom Josiah (B.1856)	Arthur (B.1859)	
Esther (B.1882)	Elizabeth (B.1858)	Albert (B.1862)	
Harry Thomas (B.1884)	Percy (B.1862)	Alice (B.1864)	
George Albert (B.1886)	Walter (B.1864)	Clara (B.1866)	
	Frank (B.1873)	Frederick (B.1867)	
		Henry (B.1871)	
		Grace (B.1878)	

ARTHUR HENRY SPIERS (B.1898) -------------------- **ANNIE JENNINGS (Queenie) (B.1901)**

Frederick Percy (B.1900)	Elizabeth Dorothy (Doll) (B.1910)
Jane Charlotte (B.1901)	Esther (B.1912)
May Rosanna (B.1903)	
Ivy Esther (B.1906)	
Dorothy (Doll) (B.1909)	
Henry George (Harry) (B.1909)	

Chapter 1: Wapping, East London – 1851

It was going to be one of those bleak, bitter-cold January mornings that only occur when you live by the river. One of those days where the grey opaque fog sucks the life out of the already weak winter sun, leaving you damp and shivering. She suspected it was going to be another gruelling day, a really gruelling day.

Sarah had woken earlier than normal. She was in pain, restless, aching, and cold. The bitter, damp wind scoffed at the pitiful attempts she had made to exclude it. She had jammed newspapers into the cracks in the window frame, but it whistled loudly as it barged in and danced around the beds in the cramped room. It attacked the sacking mattresses on the floor with the bundle of huddled-up kids and left the way it had come to torment its next victim, screaming, "Wakey, wakey." Leaving the room feeling like a crows-nest in a squall. It was still dark outside, and she wore both her cardigans over her long winter nightdress; unfortunately, as her whole wardrobe was thin and threadbare, the two cardigans only made a minor difference to her body heat. Maybe she would treat herself to some wool and knit a new one this year. She liked the vivid green the young queen had worn at Christmas, it was the height of fashion now. Sarah was a dressmaker but never quite got round to new clothes for herself; too many cold children took priority.

After bearing five children already, Sarah knew the signs. She knew today was going to be the day, she could feel it in her water, literally. She dragged out the chamber pot from under the bed and squatted awkwardly, off balance. Even when she was a girl in Kent, she hated using one, but at this time in the morning the outside privy would be frozen. The wooden seat, polished smooth by hundreds of buttocks over the years, would have ice on, the door latch would be frozen solid, and the wind would rage through the gaps in the wall, wider than the rotting timber left standing. She would have to put up with the chamber pot again. Her first husband, Samuel, teased her about her shyness. He called her Lady Sarah, and it always made her smile when she thought about him; he was the love of her life, and Sarah still missed him terribly.

She remembered fondly growing up in Bishopsbourne, a sleepy village seventy miles away in the Kent countryside within a short pony ride of Canterbury. How she met Samuel, how he courted her naively, and how their love grew with each child and deepened with the loss of their firstborn, a son who they called James but who only lived eight months. Her one consolation was that she had at least ensured he was christened. She would have been content to stay in Dover forever, with the clean sea air blowing through the loft they lived in above the sailmakers workshop. Sarah was convinced Samuel would still be by her side today if they had not been forced to find work in the damp, rat-infested hole of Stepney. After he developed lumps under his skin and subsequently died of dropsy three years ago, Sarah was left penniless with a handful of children to feed. Had Frederick not turned up that day in the tiny, cold sailmakers workshop, where would she be now? Surely she would either be in the workhouse or one of the many whorehouses on the Southbank under the authority of the Bishop of Winchester.

She was working for a pittance; she struggled to keep her head above water, to pay her rent and clothe and feed her children. The workshops were run by the collier owners. The northern England coal mine owners had the monopoly in the docks where Sarah worked; they shipped the coal in their own ships, the jobs of loading and unloading the ships were given out from the pubs, which they also owned. Gangs were selected from men who rented rooms from the landlords, they were charged inflated rent but were guaranteed work. The pit companies paid all their workers at the end of the week in their own pubs. This encouraged the men to spend a hefty chunk of their wages on beer before it ever got home to their families. Frederick Thomas Horsfall came into the sailmakers' workshop to have his battered leather jerkin repaired yet again. When Sarah looked at it, she could not help herself from laughing. "Really, luvva? I'm a stitcher, not a miracle worker. You got no more left to sew up, reckon you'll be needing a new-un." Frederick was crestfallen. He loved that jacket, he could not remember when he first got it, but he could not remember a day he had not worked in it.

What he saw that day in the dingy sweathouse was a tired lady with the last streaks of brown in her hair that were losing the battle against the advancing grey; it was neatly tied back with a cheap lamb-bone hair slide. She had blue eyes that sparkled with humour despite the conditions she found herself in. At closer inspection, he could see that the huge needles needed for the heavy sailcloth and leather were ripping her hands up. There were open sores on her palms and forefingers; this was not a trade she was born into, her hands were used to cutting and sewing dress cloth, not sail. She had only been given the job because it was her husband Samuel's beforehand, and when he had died, she lied and said she could make sails. He shyly asked her if she would go for a walk in the park on Sunday, so she could advise him on having a new one made. When she turned him down, he was like a puppy kicked into the gutter. Eyes downcast, he mumbled something about understanding, no problem, shouldn't have asked. "I got kids. Sundays the only day I get with 'em," she explained.

"Bring 'em along, be fun," Frederick blurted out unconvincingly. Sarah was enchanted. How could she refuse a man willing to spend his day off with her children and the first man for ages who had not asked her to go to a pub? The rest, as they say, is history. Although she may never love Frederick as she had Samuel, she felt safe with him, she cared for him, and she wanted more than anything else to repay his kindness and bear him the child and heir he always wanted but thought at his age was no longer a possibility.

Frederick was also married before he met Sarah – to Mary. She had not been well from their wedding day, her illness got more severe and three years after they wed, she died of consumption, leaving him alone and with more painful memories of her than treasured ones. He had only known Sarah for two years, two years that had changed his world; she brought her boisterous, sometimes screaming, sometimes arguing, always noisy children into his life and home. Even now she was pregnant, she was still amazingly full of energy and devoted to her family. At forty-nine years old, he felt

God had finally blessed him, but he did understand this was a marriage of convenience and necessity for her.

His entrance into the day was always the same, a coughing fit like a cross between the Thames foghorn and the vicar's not-so-polite cough for their attention before Sunday service at St. Georges. Sarah wondered how he never ruptured anything. It had got worse in the brief time they had been together, but whenever she mentioned it, he would say he was fine. "You just worry 'bout that fat lump you're carrying, let me worry 'bout me, girl," he would say with his lopsided toothy grin. He was no oil painting, that was for sure. He was stocky, leather-skinned and slightly stooped and bow-legged from years of lifting cargo in all weathers. It was Frederick's regular welcome to the day and his alarm call for the children; they stirred one by one, yawning, stretching, pulling on the thin cover, which in turn elicited grumbles from the others and a reciprocal tug from George, who was the biggest.

Oh, the pains; five births already and it was not any easier. This would be her last. She smiled; three times now she had vowed that, but she was not getting any younger. Forty-one was old enough to look after her four-surviving offspring, and now the new one. When George was up, she would send him to fetch Ma Murphy. She had eleven of her own and brought in every child in Charles Square for the last ten years. All the women swore by her. "Never lost one yet, least not till I got out of earshot," she used to boast with an Irish chuckle that made her whole ample body wobble.

Sarah would send the young girls to Mary to be looked after, she lived two floors down, and they would be far enough away there. George was twelve now and he had seen it all before; he knew more about newborns than Frederick, more than a lot of the women in the block come to that, but the girls should be out of the way. There would be time enough for them to learn how tough childbirth in this neighbourhood was. Then George would have to go down The Highway to the workshop where Sarah had returned as a seamstress and tell them she could not work today.

"What you doin' 'wake this time, girl?" Frederick made her jump. She had been trying to control the pain, planning the children's care and what to send with them to eat.

"Today's the day, luvva."

He looked like a cornered rat in the privy shed, his eyes darted here and there in confusion. "No! It ain't due for days," he said, "you're mistook. Besides, I got a full day's work on, there's ships stacking up downstream, what with German Albert's exhibition coming up and all."

Sarah realised at that point how much she cared for him, his childlike naivety, actually believing he would be an ounce of help if he stayed. "Best you bugger off and do what you know and leave us do what we know, don't you reckon, luvva?"

You could have seen the relief on his face from the Deptford steps across on the south bank. Frederick pulled on his heavy cotton drill trousers over his long johns and a thick horsehair shirt that looked three sizes too big. He grabbed his boots, his new leather jerkin, which still did not feel quite right, and his huge oilskin coat and ran for the door. Suddenly, he stopped, dropped them all on the floor, turned back to her, and in a couple of strides had her in his arms. "Send word with young un, soon as, eh?" Frederick then scooped up his garb and was gone. Through the spasms, Sarah found herself holding her bump and laughing. He had not even stopped for his bread and dripping for his lunch; he would regret that later.

Frederick Horsfall was a lighterman. He had loaded and unloaded ships' cargo from all over the world all his working life, from a 14-year-old apprentice to a 21-year-old Freeman of The Thames, now a 49-year-old seasoned professional, tough as old hob-nailed boots and as skilled in reading the current of the Thames as any man living. His lighter carried six ton of cargo, was flat-bottomed with one long oar that he used to steer as well. He had an apprentice boy on board learning the trade as he had. Frederick could never imagine being anything else; he loved the life of a lighterman. He was important in the dockyard hierarchy, being part of an elite guild that most of the jobbing stevedores could only dream of joining. It meant with regular work he earned thirty shillings a week, which afforded him the food, clothes, and lodgings his expanding family needed, especially now. Ships were coming in from all over the world, bringing goods and displays for the enormous exhibition planned for later in the year at the huge Crystal Palace, which had been built in Hyde Park. The world had never seen anything like this before, and Frederick was proud to be a small part in making it happen.

This year would be the best of his life: plenty of work every day on his barge, Sarah and her family, and a new baby to support. God, he hoped they were all right, he had not heard any news yet. How long did these things take? It was mid-afternoon, almost dark, and still no news.

The Thames at Wapping was a treacherous place, on a horse-shoe bend with six hundred lighters a day zigzagging from ship to shore, not to mention the watermen, who were the river taxis, plying their trade carrying captains and crew back and forth. Also, the traders crossing from the wharves of St Katherines and Wapping on the north shore to the Deptford and Woolwich docks on the south bank. The fog made it even more risky than usual. Frederick felt relieved to have got through the day unscathed, his mind had been elsewhere all day, and he was thankful it was January and dark so early. Still no message. As he manoeuvred his barge back into Bignalls yard, the old man came over. What did he want? Not now, surely? Frederick just needed to get home; something was wrong, he should have had word by now. He moored up and tied his boat to the others. "Mr Bignall, sir, is everything sweet?"

Old William Bignall stood stock still, frowning, he was always frowning. Fred thought he was born frowning. "Everything is sweet with me, young Frederick, but your life just got turned to shit."

Suddenly all his strength drained from his body, he felt weak, tired, hungry, old. He climbed out of his lighter onto the pontoon and staggered along the dockside. Was Sarah all right? He had to get home. The walk to the dock gates took an eternity, and a crowd of the other Thames lighterman were waiting for him, grinning, cheering, patting him on the back. "Congratulations, Dad, fifty-year-old, never thought you had it in you, you old git."

"Forty-nine," he said, stunned, "still only forty-nine." He was sure Old William Bignall had a hint of a smile as Frederick looked back to him.

Frederick was half carried along the ancient, cobbled road between the overhanging warehouses to The Town of Ramsgate, a long, thin, dark public house steeped in history, most of it unpleasant. The alleyway beside the tavern led to Wapping old stairs which went down to the river, the last place many convicts and sailors alike ever set foot on English soil. In fact, the cells underneath the pub were still used to house men, women and children destined for the penal colonies. A massive wooden post was visible in the mist, set deep into the foreshore where convicted pirates were chained and left for three tides to drown. Technically it was his local, even though he had only used it a couple of times. "Dark mild all-round, Jim," shouted his boss as they entered the dingy, damp bar.

When the warm, frothy beer arrived in the old pewter tankards, battered from years of use and abuse, Mr Bignall stood up on the bench, raised his mug and toasted, "To the oldest pa in Wapping, may his son be a lighterman like his old man."

Frederick's jaw went slack. *Oh my days, a boy, I've got a boy!* He was stunned; he had not even asked. "More beer, landlord. I've only bloomin' well got meself a son."

Frederick Thomas Horsfall finally met Frederick Thomas Horsfall (Jnr) when he sobered up. The boy was now one day old.

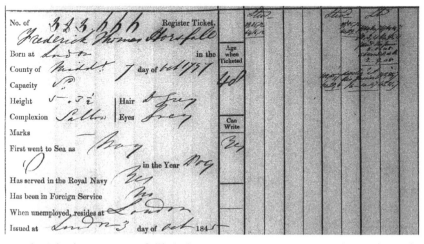

Frederick Thomas Horsfall's lighterman registration certificate (1845)

Chapter 2: Earl Shilton, Leicestershire – 1851

"Boiled chuffing turnips again?" Richard came in the back door of the small cottage smiling. He walked into the kitchen, kicked off his mud-caked boots and leant in to kiss his young bride.

She wagged a skinny carrot at him. "Don't you dare critic me cooking, or you'll end up wearing it, me ducks." Jane tried hard to look stern; however, waving a vegetable at him in mock anger did not quite have the effect she desired. They both knew March and April were called the 'hungry gap' for good reason: the months after the brassicas had finished and before the spring salads were ready, everyone in the village was in the same boat, rich or poor. She was doing the best she could to feed them with what she had available.

It was the 17th of April; tomorrow was Good Friday, and Richard had four days off from the forge. He would spend them with little James, who was nearly a year old, he was nowhere near walking, far too lazy, but his whole body shook with excitement when his father came in, arms shooting out to be picked up, squealing loudly. They would go to the village fair tomorrow and take a picnic, and he would grab a mug of beer or two: Farmer Hallam was donating a firkin. Everyone in the village would turn out, especially for the free beer. Times had been especially hard in Earl Shilton for the last ten years, the stocking-making trade that the village had thrived on was being run by a few rich landowners, who also owned the other six hundred and fifty frames that were employed in the other local villages. They were then rented to the townsfolk to work from home. However, it meant that the hosiers earnt between four and five shillings a week, where the national average was four shillings a day. Years of poverty meant an upsurge in crime, sheep stealing and even house burglary. Richard locked his front door these days, and they had nothing worth taking. Easter was a time to forget their hardships and enjoy the respite.

They awoke on Good Friday to a bright morning with warm, weak sunshine, but without the rain that had plagued the farmers' recent attempts to plant out the lettuce and pea crop, it promised to be a fine day. Richard and Jane took James and their meagre picnic, a loaf of bread, of course, they had bread with everything, it was their staple, and a small piece of cheese wrapped in a muslin cloth. They headed to the village green, where the games had been set up for the older children. The colourful cloth bunting that had originally been made for the queen's coronation had been taken out of storage yet again, and it still made a fine sight. Elizabeth was there already, perched uncomfortably on a wooden bench that had been set out for the senior ladies and the elderly men and, of course, the village dignitaries, the farmers, the frame owners, and John Green, the minister of St. Peters. Jane wore her floral dress, with little carved wooden buttons to the throat and cuffs; it was the best she had, a bit worn and faded but still better than most of the ladies would be wearing today. Elizabeth was Richard's mother, fifty-six years old and physically as frail as a sparrow chick, she looked as though a strong gust would blow her over, however one look into those hard green eyes left you in no doubt, she may be weak of body but never of mind. She was clever rather than intelligent and tough as old boots. Burying a husband and four children before her fortieth birthday would have broken many women's spirit, but it only served to strengthen Elizabeth's resolve. She was the family matriarch, make no mistake and was more akin to a hawk than a sparrow.

Richard would attempt to keep Jane and Elizabeth apart as much as possible today, and if that failed, he would retire to the beer stall and hide till things calmed down. Relations had never been good between the two women in his life, and he took full responsibility. He would love to say James was the result of a one-off roll in the hay, but the truth was that although Jane was only seventeen at the time, they had laid together many times before. Elizabeth could not forgive Jane for the sniggers she endured from the bored village wives down at Old Smock mill on wash days. Queuing to use the huge archaic mangle with their wheelbarrows full of wet clothes and nothing to do but gossip about their lifelong friends and neighbours. They had a field day when they found out Jane was expecting a child only six months after meeting Richard and before the nuptials had even been discussed, although the couple did arrange a hasty marriage when they found out Jane was pregnant. Elizabeth did not attend, of course, nor allow Richard's siblings to, and when she confided to Minister Green about Jane's condition, he refused them permission to marry in the village church. The couple married at Birdingbury, nearly twenty-five miles away, with only two strangers present to witness their union.

Elizabeth nodded curtly at Jane, and as she leant in towards James, he beamed her one of those toothless smiles which melted the old lady's heart. The past misdemeanours of her son and his wife were forgiven, just for this moment, though. She cooed at the boy squirming to escape from his mother's arms. Jane passed her son onto Elizabeth's lap but did not step back; she left her mother-in-law in no doubt that James was her son, and she would decide when and where the woman who objected so vociferously about his creation could see him.

There was an excited buzz at the Easter fair this year, not just the anticipation of the first outing of the year for the village Morris dancers; the villagers were also excited by the recent opening of the Nuneaton and Hinckley railway. The station that was due to open soon at Elmsthorpe would serve their village. They were like hungry children let loose in the strawberry fields. Already they could see the trains passing in the distance, it would not be long before they would be included in the explosion of trade the rest of the country was already benefiting from due to the extra exports to the Americas and Britain's ever-expanding empire. However, not everyone thought it was a clever idea to be connected by rail to the big cities of Birmingham, Manchester, and London. A few of the older folk in Earl Shilton had never been to Leicester, less than ten miles away, and they had no intention of travelling anywhere, certainly not London. Everything they had heard about that den of iniquity was bad news; the air was putrid, the people were thieves and robbers, even children were taught pickpocketing from birth. No, sir, their birthplace right here was by far the safest place to be.

Richard was more eager than most for the station to be opened. The train line would allow them to travel easily to wherever they wanted; for sixpence each, they could get to Birmingham and, from there, the rest of the world. He had never seen the sea, that was his first ambition. He had always been striving for a better life, and now they had a son it was even more important that he took them away from this place where nothing good ever happened, nothing exciting happened full stop. Where poor families stayed paupers for generations. Very few people in Earl Shilton had managed to raise themselves above the rank they were born into. Richard had been a labourer all his life. Firstly, in the Black Horse pub as a fifteen-year-old boy, then on the farm and now at the forge working for the blacksmith. There was more meat on the butcher's pencil, but Richard was strong as an ox and had skin the colour of a beer-soaked mahogany bar top. However, he had seen men not much older than himself turned from hardy pit ponies to stick-like hobby horses, working in the fields and barns alongside him; they were unable to stand up straight, with knee, back, elbow and finger joints so swollen they could barely lift a knife and fork, let alone guide a plough. Their disabilities left them no means to support their families except to go cap in hand to the parish poor fund. Richard would make sure Jane and their son did not ever suffer that ignominy. It was his dream to leave Earl Shilton and go as far as the new railroad would take them as soon as they could afford to do so.

1850. Marriage solemnized _by banns_ in the _Parish_ of _Barton_ in the County of _Norwich_

No.	When Married.	Name and Surname.	Age.	Condition.	Rank or Profession.	Residence at the Time of Marriage.	Father's Name and Surname.	Rank or Profession of Father.
25	April 3rd	Richard Symes	William	Bachelor	Blacksmith	Barton in the parish of Barton Norfolk	Isaiah Symes	Carpenter
		Jane Charlotte Ashworth	Minor	Spinster	servant	Barton Norfolk	Thomas Ashworth	Tailor

Married in the _Parish Church_ according to the Rites and Ceremonies of the _Established Church_ by me, _C. H. Sidwell Curate_

This Marriage was solemnized between us, { Richard Symes

William Hall

Jane Charlotte Ashworth

Charles Bartox her mark } in the Presence of us,

Richard and Jane's marriage Certificate (1850)

Chapter 3: Great Bentley, Essex – 1851

The villagers stopped their chores for half an hour in those idyllic twilight hours. They came out from their cottages or the church; they even paused their heated debates and tales of the day's labours and took their beers outside of the tiny beer houses to watch the nightly starling murmuration. The thousands of birds appeared to be a jet-black tornado, although viewed close up, each bird was a mix of blue and black, twisting and diving in perfect harmony, first one taking the lead, then without rehearsal another taking over and the flock following. The flock seemed to sense the huge expanse of grass on the largest village green in England, and it meant their acrobatic displays were visible for miles around. The fact these displays only lasted a few minutes an evening a few weeks a year made them so special to all the villagers, a treat to look forward to.

The green was surrounded by small farms, a few cottages that had been in the same families for generations and the Norman church of St Mary the Virgin that dated from the eleventh century. William could not think of a more idyllic place to live, a more perfect place to bring his sweetheart to share his life. Last week he proposed to Dianna, who he had spotted last year at the weekly market in Colchester. She was three years older than he was, and William was instantly attracted by her coquettish smile, her almond eyes, and her locks of dark, slightly uncontrollable hair. She knew she was pretty and knew the boys could not help looking at her, and she never missed the chance to wear her best dress and go to the market with her dad. The couple arranged to meet at the market every week. William took every chance he could to travel the ten miles to Colchester, and his mother, Mary Anne, knew he was besotted by someone and conveniently found a reason to send him into town every excuse she had.

Dianna had said yes, Mr Browne, her father, had said yes, and the vicar of St Mary's church in the village had agreed they could be married there, so a date had been set for next summer. William Jennings was the most contented young man in Essex.

Great Bentley was one of the oldest villages in the country, recorded in the Domesday Book with families living there for centuries. Many of the sons married their neighbours' daughters, and the families became intricately interwoven over the centuries. In times of hardship and poor harvest, brothers-in-law looked after each other, fathers provided work for nephews, and cousins supplied surplus food to their cousins. It was a sparsely populated village where most families existed with few luxuries but with all the basic necessities to live comfortable, safe, and secure lives.

Most of these necessities were paid for by an age-old, tried, and trusted system of bartering; the weekly beer tab was paid with vegetables or by sharpening a knife or supplying logs for the range. Hay for the coal horse was swapped for coal or a chicken raised in the back gardens. A burial may be exchanged for a Sunday meal or a new shirt. William's mother made gooseberry jam and honey that was coveted by everyone in the village, from tradesmen to goodwives.

William made his way back into the dark beer house owned by his father, John, and as he sat back down at the table, he heard the unmistakable drawl from the back of the pub of Holland Edenborough. "Young Ratty, I'll be wanting you down my big barn tomorrow, sharpish, got rats again in the corn store, bloody big uns. Thought you ridded 'em out last time?"

"You'll not blame me if them vermin take a fancy to your tasty corn," said William, not looking up from his pewter pot, "got a will of their own, they has."

Mr Edenborough moved across the tiny bar to loom above William. "You'd killed them like you said, they'd have trouble scrumping my stock now, don't you think?"

William looked up with a smirk. "Never said I killed 'em, just ridded ya barn of 'em."

The farmer was getting redder; the bar was now silent. No one liked Holland Edenborough; he was the biggest landowner in the area, so most of Great Bentley, Little Bentley, and the neighbouring villages relied on him for work at some time of the year. His father had married William's aunt, Rebecca Jennings, just after her father died and left her the three farms he had bought from Caius College, Cambridge, last century. The Edenboroughs' were not old money, he had married the wealthiest lady in miles, but he was no higher bred than the villagers but liked to lord it over them. "You're like your pa, always got a story, Bill Jennings."

William smirked again. "Keep your hat on yer head. I'll be there in mornin', sir." The last word emphasised for the benefit of the other drinkers, and someone sniggered, Holland Edenborough spun round to catch them but was too slow. He stomped out, shaking his head and muttering obscenities under his breath. As the heavy small oak door slammed shut, there was a coordinated expelling of breath, guffaws, a few insults, and roars of laughter.

The next day just after dawn, William took his wheelbarrow of guns, traps, and tools from the shed at the far end of their long back garden. Which was full of gooseberry bushes and fruit trees, and the beehives Mary Anne, his mother, used to make her famous honey. He went out through the newly painted white picket gate at the front of the pair of cottages with the slightly crooked pantile roofs that his father had built fourteen years ago. He had bought four plots of land from the Tendring Hundred Railway Co. for forty-nine pounds and then built the two cottages on the land using timbers from the derelict barns over at Tye Farm. It had allowed his family to move from the rowdy rooms above the beer house.

William turned right and headed down Plough Road to Aingers Green, where Holland Edenborough's rodent-infested barn was situated. He set up a brazier of jet-black pitch in the corner of the barn, lit the fire under it and waited. He could see the rats scurrying about, unfazed by his presence, some a foot long and fat. Mr Edenborough had not been exaggerating when he said they had taken over his barn. About an hour had gone by when William heard something behind him, close, breathing almost silently, but not quite, then a very slight rustle of the straw on the floor. He turned round slowly, hoping not to scare off the intruder, and he saw a pair of Topaz blue eyes staring in the dark. They were attached to a small soot-covered scamp, almost invisible in the early morning gloom. "What you doin', Ratty?"

William screwed his eyes up, put his hand on his hip and in his most serious voice said, "Well, Wally, I heard Dick Turpin was coming by this way today, an' I decided to hide in here an' protect that nice Mr Edenborough's grain store from being robbed."

Wally looked crestfallen. "Oh! I only come cos my daddy says you was catching rats."

William felt terrible. He could see the disappointment in the boy's face, so he could not tease him any longer. "Course I'm catching rats, toddler, that's why they calls me Ratty." He put his hand on the boy's head and roughly rubbed his mop of sooty hair, immediately wishing he had not. "Come sit here by the fire. I think I might have some bread in this old bag."

"With honey?" Wally said, unable to conceal his excitement.

"Course with honey, toddler, special for you." Wally was the son of John Thompson, the coal merchant, whose yard backed onto the Jennings back garden. Wally wanted to be just like William when he grew up, outside hunting rabbits, birds, and rats instead of lugging hundred-weight bags of coal all day like his own dad.

After breakfast, William and his new assistant were ready to catch rats. "There's hundreds of 'em, Ratty." Wally looked in amazement. "We gonna be here all day an' tomorrow. My mum says I gotta be home 'fore dark." Wally was now getting concerned.

"Don't you worry 'bout that, little un, pass that net."

"We really are gonna be here all day with just that net," Wally observed. He was now wondering if this had been such a clever idea. Should he have just eaten the bread and honey and gone home for breakfast with Mum? William checked his pitch pot was boiling and then slowly moved across the barn to where a particularly fat rat was nibbling at the corn pile, unafraid of the intruders. Ratty Jennings swung his net and scooped up the startled rodent. "You got one, Ratty, you got one," squealed Wally, jumping up and down, unable to hide his excitement.

"Right, you go open the barn door, Wally. Quick now." Wally did as he was told.

"What for, Ratty? We going home now?"

William gripped the squirming rat by the tail and dunked it in the hot tar, then pulled it out quickly. The screaming screech was incredible, it still made William's ears ring after years of hearing it. A loud pitched squealing that echoed round the barn and could be heard for miles. Immediately Fat Rat's death screams were heard by the other vermin in the barn, and they charged for the open barn doors, tumbling over, snapping, biting, and scratching at each other, and trampling over the slowest and youngest in their bid to escape. The terrified thieves did not stop running until they were out of earshot of their still squealing leader.

Wally was now bouncing uncontrollably, flapping his arms in the air, and screaming louder than Fat Rat in its final death throes. This was the best day of his life ever. He could not wait to tell his mum he had helped Ratty clear out a whole barn of rats and had bread with old Mrs Jennings' honey on it for breakfast.

Chapter 4: Life and Death in Blackwall – 1878

Tuesday, 3 September 1878 was a clear, fine day, blue skies and still some warmth in the late summer sun. It was a day that changed young Frederick's life forever. The paddle steamer plied her trade, carrying sightseers from London Bridge to the Rosherville Pleasure Gardens near Northfleet in Kent, where there were bear pits, caves, and ponds, along with fairground rides and all sorts of amusements. It was opened over thirty years ago and had grown into a fine place for a day trip where the air was cleaner than the city. Today's outing was advertised as a Moonlight Trip returning after dark, highlighting the sights of London, Greenwich Palace, and the Tower of London, lit by gaslights with a band and refreshments on board for only two shillings a ticket. Over nine hundred people boarded the small steamer for the return to Swan Pier at London Bridge, but no one was really counting. The crew knew she was near capacity as she sat low in the water, and every seat and space both below deck and around the upper deck rails was full of tired but still excited passengers. Mainly women and children, as it was a weekday, in their Sunday best long dresses and smart suits. They pointed out landmarks to each other and were still cheering passing boats and waving to people on the shore as the band played on the foredeck. Many commented on the sudden stench from the river as they approached Barking. Twice daily at an hour after high tide, the sewage plants in Barking on the north shore and Woolwich to the south discharged seventy-five million gallons of raw sewage into the Thames to be washed downstream to the sea. The sewage gates had been opened an hour earlier, so the smell was at its worst. It was a little after seven thirty in the evening and just about dark when the SS *Princess Alice* rounded Gallions Reach in Barking, a hairpin bend in the river. The helmsman cut the corner to take the shortest route as a huge black hulk loomed toward them. The *Bywell Castle* was an eight-hundred-and-ninety-ton collier, three times as heavy as the pleasure boat. It was only carrying a minimal amount of ballast and was sitting high in the water as it headed back to Newcastle to reload with coal. Both captains ordered full reverse thrust but were too late to avoid the *Bywell Castle* ploughing into the mid-ships of the *Princess Alice* behind the paddle box and slicing her in half.

Five minutes after the impact, the *Alice* had sunk completely, throwing all those on the upper decks into the river, trapping all those below decks and taking them under the filthy water to their deaths. The Thames was throbbing with thrashing, screaming ladies in heavy long dresses being dragged under, with their children, most unable to swim, flailing helplessly around them. Witnesses stated that had it not been for the sewage, many more passengers and crew may have survived, instead they choked to death on untreated effluent. The water was described by an eyewitness as a bubbling cauldron of acid and filth. Of the one hundred and thirty who did survive the water and were taken to Woolwich infirmary, thirty died within days from poisoning. Sixty-two bodies were recovered that were never claimed or identified.

The following day, all river boatmen, both watermen and lightermen, were offered two pounds a day payment and five shillings for each body they recovered. Frederick Horsfall joined them. For those who worked on the Thames, dead bodies were a common occurrence. Maybe ship hands bound to their captains, who had jumped ship when they had reached port in a failed attempt to escape, or drunken sailors fallen in the river by accident or maybe killed in a fight and dumped in the easiest place, or even young women who had been defiled, who felt suicide was their only escape and had jumped from a bridge. In the days immediately following the disaster, the dead were plentiful, and all the boatmen earnt well. Over eighty bodies were laid out at the Royal Victoria Gardens at Cyprus on the north bank of the Thames for families to come and claim. More bodies were taken to the town hall at Woolwich, to the south. As the river became clear of the dead, the arguments started between the boatmen as to who had the right to a final bloated, decaying corpse, stained with sewage and washed up on the shore or released from the unstable wreck on the tide to float to the surface. This led to fights between the rivermen over the last remaining bounty.

Frederick Thomas Horsfall was twenty-seven years old and had not seen scenes like this in the thirteen years he had been a lighterman. He had witnessed the opposite, both camaraderie and support, his father had died when he was still a boy. The support of the lighterman guild when he came of age to apprentice, honouring his father's lighterman service and allowing his son to join the guild. William Bignall's company had sponsored the fourteen-year-old apprentice in his father's memory. For him to witness lightermen and watermen who lived together, drunk together and prayed together, fighting over corpses while the city still mourned, was too much for Frederick to ever forget.

Since Frederick became a Freeman Thames lighterman with Bignall's at Blackwall Point and he had worked the East India Docks, his life had been good. He had met Charlotte seven years ago when he was twenty; she was three years older than him but looked much younger. Charlotte was elfin-faced, she had bright, alert brown eyes and black hair, which she kept unfashionably short, and she smiled easily and often. She was quiet, but she noticed everything. She spoke softly and without any confidence; often she could not think of the word she wanted and ended up not finishing her sentence at all. Frederick found this endearing, and because he did not laugh at her, as her siblings had always done, she was comfortable in his company. After only six months courtship, they married, a union that had so far produced three children. The youngest, a son, who Frederick had always hoped would follow himself, his father and his grandfather into the lighterman trade. After the events of today, he was not sure that was a sensible idea anymore.

Three children from the same parents could not have been more physically different. Charlotte, the eldest at five years old, was a carbon copy of her mother, petite with a pale, doll-like complexion and quiet. She had the same dark hair, maybe a little longer than her mother's and always kept tied back neatly. Charlotte did not have a problem learning words, though she preferred not to talk. Then there was Florence, a little over two years old, she had been repeating every word she heard parrot fashion for a year now. "Jabber, jabber, jabber, that all that girl can do?" Frederick used to mock her mother when he came home tired and cold. Florence would jump on his lap while he was still trying to unlace his boots. She would tell her pa everything that happened in their house that day as fast as she could tumble the words out. Often, if something exciting had occurred, if the rent man had called or if Ma had made cakes, her relating of the day's events would turn into a shrieking, bouncing, arm-waving performance, pleading with her mother and sister to confirm her tale was true. It usually ended with her dragging Frederick by the hand, one boot on, one boot off into the kitchen to prove to him that there really were homemade cakes or the rent money had gone from the tin. As for her looks, Florence, although younger than her sister, was already taller. She was heavier, with long, pale brown hair that was always unkempt. Immediately after her hair had been brushed and tied up, the ribbon would be hanging adrift, and she would look like the milkman's horse had dragged her halfway along the Old Highway. While her sister Charlotte would keep her dress clean for days, Florence could not keep hers clean for more than an hour. Baby Frederick was quiet like his eldest sister, a calm, content child but dark-haired and dark-skinned from his father's side of the family. Even at that early age, Charlotte, Florence, and Frederick were developing a love and trust that would carry them through the rest of their lives.

One constant for all the children was the evening ritual of reading. After tea, Frederick sat down with a copy of the *Illustrated London News*, a daily newspaper that also had pictures which kept the children interested. One girl sat on each leg. At first, he read to them, then as they got older, he listened while they read to him. As the years went on, more children came, and his lap was too small to accommodate them all, so they sat at the kitchen table with the paraffin lamp giving off just enough light to read by in winter. He had learnt to read and write himself this way, with his mother and his Sunday school teacher helping. Although his mother could barely read herself and hardly write at all. Back then, schooling was not compulsory as it was now, from five years old. He believed it was the most important thing in the world to teach children to read. "Never need trust what no one tell yer agin when yer can read yersels."

Charlotte had started going to Prestons' infant school when she was five years old but could already read a lot of the words in the newspaper herself, and Frederick used to correct the long words or names she had not seen before. Florence began by copying what Charlotte said until her sister shouted, "Pa, tell 'er, tell 'er, I'm trying to constonstate."

"Enough, Florrie, your turn in a minute. Let Charlotte alone to read; she's constonstating," he would say, trying to hide his grin.

After Florrie had her turn and they had finished, and Frederick's legs had lost all feeling, the girls would jump up and down shouting, "Say it, Pa, say it."

"All right, all right, settle down, little 'uns. Nuff red, nuff sed, time fer yerz off to yer bed." Florence thought this was the funniest bit of her day, every day.

The moment the *Bywell Castle* collided with the *Princess Alice*, as reported in the *London Illustrated* (1878)

River boatmen collecting the bodies from the Thames in the days after the disaster, as reported in the *London Illustrated* (1878)

Chapter 5: Running Away – 1878

Richard was now fifty-four; he and Jane had talked of leaving so many times, running away to a more exciting life outside their constricting village. Every time they believed the time was right to leave Earl Shilton, something hindered them, either an unexpected addition or a tragic loss to their family; Elizabeth, their tiny daughter, had died when she was not yet a year old, and the long-term illness of Richard's mother, also called Elizabeth, finally took her life. Eventually, the collapse of the already fragile, outdated stocking-making industry was the last straw. The home-working local economy had been in decline for decades, but the blockading of the American ports by the Unionist troops put the final nail in the coffin. Leicestershire's home-working stocking trade never recovered, and factories in the towns took over; they manufactured stockings much quicker and cheaper than outworkers. The requirement for blacksmithing declined as a result, fewer carts were required and, in turn, fewer horseshoes and saddlery. The blacksmith he was working for had no choice but to let him go. It left Richard little choice but to leave the village he was born in, grew up in and had started to raise his family in. Within a month he had packed up his remaining seven children, his beloved wife of twenty years and a wooden trunk containing all the possessions they owned and headed to the train station for a new life in Birmingham. It was apparent very soon that the move was not the adventure they expected; his job as a night watchman paid barely enough to keep his brood fed and housed, let alone to save for his ambition to see the sea.

"Walt, Art, where are yous pesty kids, get yousells in 'ere." Richard called the boys in for dinner the same way every day.

"And me, Pa, don't forget me, I'm here too."

"You're not a pesty kid, ducks, you're pa's special girl." Richard hugged Elizabeth's red hair to his face. She was now

twenty years old; she really was his special child. She had been
given the same name as her dead sister, who was originally named
after Richard's mother. She and John held a space in his heart
unlike the others. John was their second born, James was older
and now lived away from home, but John looked like his father,
walked like his father, had the same sense of humour, he acted like
a younger version of Richard. He could not have been prouder
of his boy, well, not so much a boy, twenty-six years old now.
John worked as a fireman on the railway, travelling all over the
country, shovelling coal into that insatiable steel mouth, gaping
like the door to Hades. Richard envied his son's lifestyle, seeing
parts of the country he could only dream of visiting, Liverpool,
Manchester; he even went to London once. Richard made him tell
them every detail. What were the people like? Were they friendly?
How big was it? John was awestruck, he tried to describe London,
but he had nothing to compare it to. He told of the docks and
the hundreds of ships he had seen, and the palaces, and, of course,
Big Ben. That just convinced Richard even more that one day he
would leave Aston and see it for himself.

The work was hard at first. John thought his muscles would rip
away from his bones, but now after eight years, his shoulders were
so broad his father could not clasp his arms around them and link
his fingers. John could lift all of his brothers at the same time in
a bear hug, although Jane scolded him every time, "John, you big
lump, you'll squash them poor boys to bits, now put them down."
She would whack him with whatever she was holding at the time in
a vain attempt to keep some semblance of parental control. He
would drop the boys and lift her like a rag doll and spin her around
laughing, the same way Richard used to in their courting days.

"Richard, will you control this lump of yours?" she would
implore, sweeping her hair back and smoothing down her flour-
covered apron, trying to look stern, but it always ended in fits of
laughter.

"So where is the big fella tonight, my precious? Is he coming
home for food?"

"Said he was this mornen, ducks," Jane answered without
looking up from the pot she was stirring on the hearth.

"Reckon he's with that floozie Dot again or Maisy or that posh one from Solihull," said Arthur.

"Lucky sod," giggled Walt.

"That's enough, all of you, in front of your sister an all." Jane cast a fierce look at the boys, and they knew they would face a wooden spoon if they uttered another word. She ladled the thick stew into the metal bowls and handed them round. First Richard, then Elizabeth, and then the boys, who were still grinning and whispering innuendos to each other. She served her sons in strict order of age, a ritual she had learnt as a child from her father, who had spent twenty years in the army.

Richard cut thick doorsteps of the coarse, hard-crusted bread; he took one and pushed the board across the table. "Don't snatch, Art, pass one to yous sister, 'an leave some for our John."

Jane enjoyed this part of the day the most, the satisfied slurping, munching, and crunching mixed with excited talking with mouths half full, relating their day's news. Her children believed they were the first to ever experience the sights and smells of daily life, the canal barges pulled by enormous trudging horses, the factories spewing noxious gas into the air or the pickpockets or beggars. Richard listened as though they were intrepid explorers retelling tales of unheard-of tribes or distant lands; he still dreamt of being that explorer. He remembered not so long ago being awed himself by the filth and poverty of his new surroundings, the depths men and women sunk to in order to feed their families. The poverty in Earl Shilton was still poverty, but the degradation and filth here took him years to accept as normal. He had never come to terms with the shabby street ladies selling themselves to support their children or to buy gin to give them courage enough to resell their bodies again tomorrow. This was new for him; apart from Sally Lunt back in his old village, a young widow who charged men for the service, although most of the village women suspected she did it more for her pleasure than the little money she earnt.

The din of the family meal was interrupted by a loud banging on the back door. They all looked at Richard, who stood up. "It's all right, finish your food." The sight that met him drained all colour from his weather-beaten face. John was hanging limp, his arms draped across two strangers shoulders, his face dropped to his chest. Richard's first thought was, *Thank the lord, he is not bleeding.* "Bring him in. What in Jesus' name has happened to him?"

The two men carried him to the bed in the front room. Jane was right there. "John, John, what's 'appened to yous? John, it's Ma, talk to me."

One of the men, the older of the two, was covered in coal dust; it was the other who spoke first, "Sorry, lady, we was working in the yard when he staggers in from the rail yard like what he is now, my mate Nat here knew him from the pub on the corner, so we lifted him round here like."

The two men said they were sorry at least three more times and then left. Richard never did find out the elder man's name. Jane sent Arthur to fetch the doctor. Arthur told him John was coughing more than breathing, he did not have the strength to lift his own arms, let alone lift his brothers up. He had left for work a giant and returned home a ragdoll.

Doctor Anderson was a corpulent Scot in his fifties but looked ten years older. His extended belly reminded Arthur of their heavily pregnant neighbour, and he was red-faced and rarely sober. His old, worn and stained jacket hung on the back of the chair; his shirt sleeves were creased, but in contrast his gold watch chain was gleaming against the black threadbare waistcoat. He listened to Arthur's list of symptoms without looking up from his dinner plate. "Tell yer mam I'll be there shortly, son."

"But my mother said..." replied Arthur before his imploring was cut off with a glare. The doctor forced a large forkful of food into his mouth, immediately followed by a glug of wine. Arthur watched a small dribble of red liquid escape from the corner of the doctor's mouth. He ran back home to report to the family as fast as he could.

The Scottish doctor arrived ninety minutes later. He nodded curtly to Richard and examined John while Jane hysterically recounted the evening's drama. He felt his pulse, took out his stethoscope and listened to John's breathing, weak as it was. He stood, straightened his waistcoat, assuming that somehow he now looked respectable and announced John had consumption.

A seven-minute visit, a shilling charged, and news that changed their lives forever.

John died a week later in the same bed in Aston that he had been placed on by Nat and his un-named friend. He was twenty-six years old.

The railway company that had employed John sent Dr John Lloyd to confirm his cause of death and sign the certificate; he diagnosed chronic peritonitis as the cause of John's sudden demise. Richard and Jane buried their son four days later. They had been through child loss before, but this time was different; John was not a baby. Richard's entire world had been torn apart as though he had been repeatedly beaten in the stomach with a knuckle duster, and he now found it impossible to concentrate on anything apart from his dead boy.

He sat in silence with his head resting on his fist, lost in the thoughts going round his head, transfixed at the changing scenery unfolding outside the grimy train window. Alternating from the grey industrial cityscape of Birmingham to the green rolling Warwickshire countryside then back to the smoking chimneys of Coventry and on southwards, through Northamptonshire and Bedfordshire and eventually into London. Richard and Jane had finally managed to escape with some of their family away from the smog and the constant noise that Birmingham produced. The hammering of the factories, the shouting of the labourers, and the squealing of the train brakes shunting in and out of the sidings. Dust and smoke hung in the air, the unmistakable smell of hydraulic engine oil that permeated every pore of skin, every scrap of clothing of every man, woman, and child who came in contact with it. No matter how many times they tried to scrub the pungent odour of the city out of their lives, it hung on like a limpet.

He was barely conscious of the gentle rat-a-tat of the huge metal wheels on the tracks, the rattling of the ill-fitting carriage doors, his excited family sitting in the long open carriage shuffling uncomfortably on the hard oak slatted seats. The constant hiss of the steam engine and the occasional shrieking whistle punctuated the idyll that should have been the trip of his dreams. His thoughts were still with John, what he would have thought of their journey, how he would be teasing his siblings. He would be punching his father on the arm. "Well done, Dad. Yous did it. Yous dreams finally coming about." Richard realised for the first time he missed the bruises on his arms. John would be telling them all about the route, how much longer to London, what to expect around the next bend. As he caught his reflection in the dusty glass, Richard realised the last months had taken their toll on him: he looked weary, he was tired, he felt old.

Jane was watching the soulless expression on his face. She remembered the animated childlike grin he had whenever he talked about this moment, the odyssey he had dreamt of for so many years; she smiled when she thought back to those early days together in Earl Shilton. Unfortunately, she had seen the vacant stare he now had so many times recently; she knew what he was thinking, she was thinking it too. She slid her gloved hand into his but said nothing. He turned his head slightly to glance at her reflection in the window, but she could not meet his eyes and lowered her face. The pain they could see in each other's faces was still too much to acknowledge.

"Ma, will yous tell tha' bloody nuisance to git a rest."

Jane swivelled round towards them. "Haven' I told yous not to say that word, Arthur? Be nice to yous brother."

Frank was so excited, he had never left the city before, he could see for miles, the fields were amazing, he had never seen a real cow in a real field with real grass, in the countryside before. He was too young when they left Earl Shilton to remember the fields. He had only seen them in the Bull Ring on the Thursday market, and then he remembered his brothers had great fun telling him what was going to happen to the cattle being sold for slaughter, he was always more sensitive than the others. Frank missed John, of course he did, but he missed Elizabeth too, who had stayed behind in Aston. Her marriage had been a bit of a rush, but she had decided she did not want to leave. All Ma and Pa talked about was John this, John that. This was new, he could feel it for all of them; they needed to leave behind the claustrophobic presence of their brother in their little house in Aston. He could not understand why they all looked so sad. This was the most exciting day of his life.

Arthur secretly wished he could bounce up and down on the seat every time he saw something new, but somehow, he felt it was disrespectful and inappropriate. The other brothers felt the same. They were beginning to shake off the shackles of Birmingham, and this was their only chance to escape the city they had all grown to despise. The boy's enthusiasm was infectious. With every new field, every free-flowing river they crossed, each new wonder they experienced, the mood lightened, and the older brothers smiled a little more. Jane leant into Richard a little and gripped his hand a little tighter; she even thought at one point he stifled a grin when Walter slipped off the seat. He was eager to catch a second glimpse of a pretty girl in a blue dress who had long, blond hair and was waiting at a road crossing with her scruffy looking dog. Arthur laughed uncontrollably, Frank too. Walter eventually grinned, they realised this was the first time that the whole family had laughed together since John had been brought home.

The last four hours of the journey to London were filled with questions, answers, excitement, and promises. Richard remembered the enthusiasm he had once felt for this life-changing journey. The weight felt lifted from his shoulders, and he felt the relief at having finally taken this decision, a decision he took for the future of his family. Their lives would start anew in that carriage, right now. He felt immense pride in his family today, the resilience they had shown coping with their loss and coming out the other side with their sense of humour and ambition still intact. Arthur later recalled that the rest of that train ride was the happiest he had ever felt before.

The Spires family arrived at Kings Cross station in London late on that Thursday night, tired and hungry. The last thing they wanted to do was to sleep, but London would still be there tomorrow, they would explore it then.

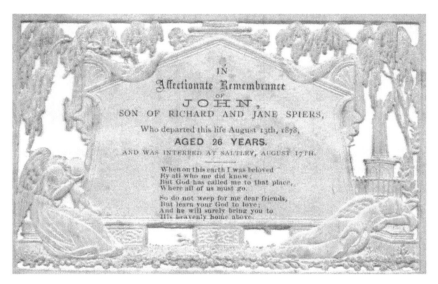

John Spiers remembrance card (1878)

Chapter 6: SS *Waroonga* – 1885

The third Christmas his family had spent in London had come and gone, and while his children all seemed content with their new lives, Richard was itching to get going. He knew if they got settled here, they may never complete the final leg of their journey. The money he bought with him had gone on board and lodging two years ago. Living in London was so much more expensive than Aston. They had all struggled to find regular work, a few days in the docks here and there, maybe a day or two labouring or cleaning, just enough to keep them fed and sheltered. Richard had been to see the Queensland agent-general; he had queued for two days outside his office in the Strand before being seen. The Australia agent, a small, neat man with an equally small, neat moustache, had agreed to have the family's fares paid in full as part of the new assisted migration programme that had been set up to help families start a new life in the territory. It was vital for Australia's economy to send people from England to work the land, and Richard was a blacksmith by trade, although it had been some years since he had worked a forge.

It had been seventeen years now since convicts were last transported, and the country desperately needed fresh labour. However, the migration system was painfully slow and corrupt. The agent-general first had to be convinced the families were fit enough to survive the long, tortuous journey and they knew what to expect from the incredibly demanding conditions when they finally arrived. Also, he had to be sure they were committed to the long-term development of England's latest colony. When he was sure an applicant fulfilled all the criteria, transport then had to be arranged. A whole new trade was growing in shipping migrants to Australia. However, most of the old sailing ships from the now redundant convict trade had been re-purposed, and new steamers were taking their place slowly. There were still many experienced crew who had covered the journey numerous times and knew the safe harbours and victuallers along the route, waiting for ships to become available. A ship's captain would obviously prioritise those passengers who could pay their passage, then fill his ship afterwards with families from the assisted migration scheme, which paid him much less. Jane suspected the agent and his deputy were accepting bribes to send some families on before them. Richard thought Jane just did not like the two men. Richard did not like them either. The agent spelt his name as it sounded in Richard's midlands accent. It had happened occasionally in the past, and as Richard was illiterate, it was never corrected; the Spires family became Spiers permanently with one stroke of his pen.

"What yous doing, our lass?"

"Whassit to do with you? An' I ain't your lass," the girl said, tugging her wayward locks behind her ear in an attempt to look a little less bedraggled and more in control.

Arthur apologised, "Sorry, I see yous jest sitting there, looking at nowt, wondered what yous doing, I did." It was only late February, but spring was coming early this year, not quite arrived yet but definitely on its way. A few white fluffy clouds blotted the otherwise perfect pale blue sky. The sun looked as though it should be warm, but it could not be bothered this early in the year, it was saving itself for summer. The sun was giving off a bright light but not much heat; she thought it was like the new electric lights they had put up a couple of years ago, which she saw when she went to the West End. She had her green, heavy winter coat on, but the big black buttons were undone, and her hands were thrust firmly in the pockets.

She reclined her head and rested it on the back of the park bench and closed her eyes. "Yer still 'ere?"

He had sat down on the bench and was watching her intently. "Me? No, I gone, I has."

"Don't flippin sound like yer 'as to me, sounds like I've tell'd yer to bugger off an yer still 'ere." He grinned; he liked this scruffy girl. About his age, he reckoned from her size. Local, definitely local, had the look, the accent, the attitude. "What's so funny with yer then?" she said, still with her eyes shut.

"How yous do that, know I'm smiling when yous has yous eyes shut? My ma does that, knows when I's snitching bread even when she's dozing."

"Probably on 'count o' yer bein' so clumsy." They sat in silence for a few minutes, her pretending to sleep in the sunshine, him transfixed by her.

She opened her eyes and caught him staring, he apologised again. "Sorry, yous alright? Yous look sad like."

"There ain't nuffink wrong with me, an wots all the 'yous' about anyways? What's 'yous' even mean? Where did yer learn not to talk proper?"

"That's rich coming from yous, blowse. Tis better than 'yer', no one never heard that said nowhere ever."

She suddenly turned towards him. She looked angry, and he thought she was going to punch him. Arthur put his hands up dramatically to fend off the blow. "Blowse am I? I'll give yer a four-penny one, then we'll see who's a blowse." She tried hard to act angry, but she was grinning as she slapped him.

They sat on the battered wooden bench overlooking the river and talked and laughed and talked some more. He told her about Birmingham and his train journey here, and she talked about her family. And about her love of reading. He could read, but he did not enjoy it, he was better with numbers. Arthur's hands were clamped between his knees, and she still had hers fixed inside her green coat, taking them out only to tease a wayward wisp of hair back behind her ear. It was a never-ending task, no sooner had she tidied it than it fell back across her face. Arthur thought it was the most endearing thing he had ever seen. Once he stroked her hair back in place for her, she glared at him, and he did not do that again.

"I gonna see yer again?" she suddenly asked, looking straight at him. He hesitated. That was the response she dreaded; she knew it was too good to be true. Someone she liked, someone who made her laugh, but he did not want to see her again. Just her luck. She jumped up with a theatrical flounce of her long, unruly hair and headed toward the park gate; she did not look back. Tears started to well up, and she was not sure if it was anger or regret.

"Stop, no wait, stop, no stop, please let me tell yous," he implored, running after her, grabbing her arm.

"Nuffink to tell, I reckon," she said with her eyes downcast, still not looking at him.

He brushed a tear from her face. "No, there is. I wanna see yous agin, I do, but thing is—"

"There's always a 'thing is', ain't there?" she interrupted him angrily.

"No, really, thing is, me an' my folks are off to Australia next week. We got our papers through see, we been waiting years for this like I told yous."

The scruffy girl with the big attitude stared into his face, checking him out, she had grown up with enough wrong 'uns to tell. He looked like he was telling her the truth, and she wanted him to be telling her the truth. "Yer really thinks I'm a blowse, though?"

"Aye, the prettiest one I ever seen." He got another slap for that.

Arthur did meet the girl on the bench one more time the day before he sailed. He realised he had not even asked her name, she told him, and she told him where she lived. He told her what ship he was sailing on, and they both knew they would never meet again. He wanted to kiss her goodbye, but he did not. She wished he had; she had tied her hair up neatly with a green ribbon for him.

The SS *Waroonga* was only built two years before. Three hundred and fifteen feet of steel and steam, purposely designed to carry passengers and cargo to the other side of the world. Ships like her were built to replace the old wooden sailing ships that had been used as convict carriers, where living, eating, and sleeping in comfort had not been the designer's priority. The old sailing ships took two months longer to get to Australia, and because of the conditions on board, many more convicts died on the arduous journey. The new steamships had a surgeon and a matron on board, primarily to ensure the health and wellbeing of the paying passengers, of course, but the free boarders and crew were also well cared for. The matron's main responsibility was to care for the single women and ensure their safe arrival. There were over a hundred and sixty single women on board this trip, mainly listed on the ship's manifest as domestic servants. These women were travelling to the other side of the world in search of a new life and a new husband. Most came from Ireland or Scotland, where the harvests had been so poor over the past few years and had never recovered fully from the devastating famine in 1879. Their families could not afford to feed them, so had no choice but to send them to the new worlds of America or Australia in the hope they could find a better life. Australia had a surplus of men; there were over two million people there already, predominantly males. There were ex-convicts, now released, having served their seven-year transportation sentences. Soldiers originally sent to guard them, who decided to stay. Farmers and labourers, and since 1851, an estimated one million gold prospectors had arrived in the new country from all around the world, all with the same aim: to make their fortune.

Richard could not believe it; he stood on the wooden jetty at Tower Bridge pier and gazed at the steel hulk before him. He had spent so many years dreaming of this moment, and now it was within his grasp. He thought of all the people over the years who doubted his resolve. His family in Earl Shilton who thought he was mad to leave his safe little village to go as far as Birmingham. His neighbours in Aston who envied his ambition but thought it was a pipe dream. He thought of John, who should have been here sharing this moment with them, and tears filled his eyes. Jane gently rubbed the back of his neck; they all knew what this day meant to him. Today was the culmination of his whole life's dream. It was his dream; the rest of his family were essential extras, but it was his dream. He was convinced his sons and all their future generations were the ones who would live to benefit from his ambition. "Come on, duck, yous don't wanna miss the boat now yous this close."

He rubbed his eyes with the back of his hand. "What yous lot all standing about here for, it'll not get us boarded like this," he said. He grinned like a naughty schoolboy.

There were one hundred and sixty-six passengers who were not fee-paying; the other two hundred and eighty-six were all paying various amounts, so the free ones were loaded first with the cargo. They would have the longest time to wait before sailing. Richard was faced on the gangway by a smartly dressed first mate with a thick blue cotton top and matching trousers. He appeared around the same age as Richard, but he was stocky where Richard was wiry. He was certainly not fat, but he looked as though twenty years ago he would have been a bull of a man. He had a perfectly round bald head like a white cannonball, a moustache that he was growing in the popular Chinese style, combed across under his nose with thin strips down the sides joining a goatee beard. Jane was impressed it was still jet black, and when she looked again, she realised his eyebrows were also black, perhaps he was not as old as his weathered face portrayed. When he spoke, his accent sounded Russian, but they learnt later he was Crimean. He checked their boarding papers carefully, then said, "We take you to mess, you sleep, eat, and wash there. You not go anywhere else on ship. Understand, ya? When you done jobs, you come here if you want air, only here, this deck, nowhere else. Understand, ya? No talk to big passengers or young girls on ship." He looked straight at the three boys when he said this, and they shook their heads in unison. Jane wondered if she could perfect that accent so her sons would be as compliant for her. "Leave trunk here, it go in hold," he ordered. They each had a bundle of clothes, bedding and eating utensils with them, as they had been instructed; the rest of their possessions they would see again when they docked. They followed a young crewman down thin metal steps into the bowels of the ship, past the small galley where they would prepare their own food and past the small toilet for their mess rooms use.

The space they were allocated had three rows of three bunks on each wall, with a long table and benches running down the middle. This would be their world for the next two months. Two men were already sitting on bunks at the end of the small room; they nodded and mumbled a greeting. Jane put her blanket on a top bunk at the other end of the mess. Richard put his on the bunk underneath, with the boys taking the ones next to them. During the next hours, the other eleven emigrants joined their little group, two young couples nervously introduced themselves, the rest were single men. All joined in their excitement of their forthcoming adventure, but at the same time praying the others would be decent travelling companions for the next two months. Arthur lay on his mattress, staring at the bunk above him. This was supposed to be the most exciting day of his life, so why was he not feeling it? He could not stop thinking of the scruffy girl in the park. How ridiculous, they had only met twice.

The *Waroonga* set sail with the dawn tide on the morning of 10 March 1885. The girl leant on a jetty post wrapped in her green coat with its big black buttons. Her fists clenched tightly, stretching the pockets, and a pink knitted hat pulled down over her ears to ward off the early morning chill. Her hair was fighting to escape its confines, and it had succeeded over her left ear; she could feel a few damp strands brushing her face but had no mind to deprive it of its freedom this morning. She watched the ship gently leave its berth, the shouts of the crew confirming the ropes were clear, a few passengers hanging over the rail, but they were too well dressed to be him. She was not sure why she was even there; did she really expect the stupid Brummie boy not to have left on it?

Within an hour of sailing, the ship was gently rocking. Two of the other men in their mess were Irish and had been on a ship before when they came to London. They grinned as they assured the others this was nothing. They had not even reached the open sea yet, and it would get far worse. None of the other passengers knew what to expect. They ate their first meal afloat, working out how to keep the plates on the table and their backsides on the benches. After clearing the table and tidying their bunks, the steerage passengers were permitted on deck. They rounded the Thames estuary and sailed out into the English Channel, by which time the tide had changed. The gentle swell of the Thames had become white-capped breakers rocking the ship. Most of the virgin seafarers lost their breakfast long before they passed the White Cliffs and their last sight of England, much to the amusement of the crew who had gathered on deck waiting for this spectacle. The passengers got their first lesson in seamanship that morning, afterwards they always checked which direction the wind was blowing before leaning over the gunwale to throw up.

The daily ritual on board was always the same: up at 6am, wash, dress, prepare and eat breakfast. Then cleaning, scrubbing, and washing everything that stood still. Clothes, floors, walls, and bedding, not to mention the decks. In the afternoon, if the chores had been carried out to the satisfaction of the first mate who they had met on their first day onboard, the travellers were allowed recreation time, either on deck or in their own mess room. This was the time many used to read or write a journal if they were literate, to play cards or games, although gambling was strictly forbidden. After leisure time, they prepared and ate dinner, more tidying up and cleaning and lights out at 10pm. Followed by the same routine the next day. After the first few days, the seasickness abated in most of the passengers, and life on board ship was becoming normal, then the *Waroonga* entered the Bay of Biscay. Even a few of the seasoned crew succumbed to seasickness this time, although the captain forbade them to let any passenger witness this on punishment of a day's pay. Some passengers were unable to leave their bunks, many were unable to leave the mess room or cabin they were allocated, the lucky few made it on deck. Cleaning and scrubbing were particularly vigilant throughout the whole ship for the next few days. Frank was heard to grumble that if he were a convict, he would have been chained up and would not have been forced to do jobs every day.

The following days were a respite for all on board. After the Straits of Gibraltar, the Mediterranean was benign compared to the Atlantic. Then they had the Suez Canal to navigate, a modern feat of engineering they had all heard about, which saved nearly a month on the trip. After which, the first port of call was Aden, a chance to get the trunk out of the hold and change clothes or add anything forgotten initially. Also, a brief opportunity to stretch their legs on dry land. To wonder in awe at the sights and smells of a different world. The ship was in dock for two days to restock with fresh water and food, and the coal bunkers were refilled by local labourers for the next leg of the journey. It was at this point that William Carney, a fee-paying passenger, was taken and left ashore; he was diagnosed with smallpox, the first casualty of the journey since Maria Reder from Holstein had died after only three days at sea.

After Aden, the routine on board continued as before during the next leg to Columbo in Ceylon, except for one small drama. Well, two actually, the births of two baby girls. One was named Francis Hume, and the other, born a week later, was named by her mother, Margaret Waroonga Loughlin. Although not unusual, the two births at sea served to remind the passengers that life on board and ultimately life at their final destination would still continue as before, maybe not as they had previously known, but what would become their new normal. Everyone on board had been disturbed by the serious illness of William Carney, they knew the chances of him surviving were minimal, so the births boosted the ship's morale. The remaining weeks of the journey were completed with the same cleaning, eating, cleaning, reading, sleeping boredom they had endured since they left London.

They eventually docked in the sweltering heat of Brisbane on Wednesday, 6 May 1885, eight weeks after leaving a damp, grey London. The SS *Waroonga* unloaded four hundred and sixty-two passengers and two exceedingly small babies onto the farthest point of the British empire. Richard, Jane, Frank, Walter, and Arthur Spiers had achieved the impossible family dream.

140 — *Waroonga*

No.	Surname	Christian Name	Age										Occupation
		Remittance Continued		3	3	10	12	8	6	1	1		
3872	Mann	Elizabeth	4						1				
3220	McCabe	Pat	46	1		1							Bookbe...
"	"	James	25			1							
3714	McLeod	James	18			1							Farm...
3789	McCarthy	James	20			1							Labor
3060	Mitchell	Winifred	18					1					Dom...
3872	Morgan	Catherine	19					1					
3060	Mitchell	John	26			1							Farm
2900	McDonnell	Edward	20			1							
2257	Markey	Thomas	33			1			■				Carpen...
3716	O'Neill	Thomas	23			1							Farm
3100	Phillip	John	21			1							
3852	Tegg	Charles G.	23			1							Farm
3160	Reynolds	Mick	20			1							Farm
"	"	James	19			1							
"	"	Pat	17			1							
2841	Rapier	Elizabeth	21					1					Dom...
2889	Reilly	Martin	22			1							Farm
3650	Russell	John	47	1									Cler...
"	"	Margaret	40	1	1								
3725	Ryan	Margaret	18					1					Dom...
"	"	Mick	48	1	1								Labor
"	"	Mary	48	1	1								
"	"	Daniel	9						1				
2841	Rapier	Christopher	16			1							Labor
2269	Smith	John G.	19			1							Farm
3663	Spiers	Richard	49	1	1								Black...
"	"	Jane	39		1								
"	"	Frank	11						1				
"	"	Walter	20			1							Labor
"	"	Arthur	16			1							
3721	Stewart	David	38	1									
"	"	Mary	38		1								
"	"	William	5						1				
"	"	James	3						1				
"	"	Jane	1								1		
3124	Shapcott	William	26			1							Pattern...

SS *Waroonga* ship's manifest (March 1885)

														COUNTY OR COUNTRY	REMARKS
7	9		9												
										No	No	P.	York	
				1					Yes	Yes	R.C.	Monaghan	
				1					"	"			
1									"	"	P.	Forfar	
									"	"			
				1					"	"	R.C.	Sligo	
									"	"	P.	Glamorgan	
				1					"	"	R.C.	Sligo	
				1					No	No	"	Kings Co	
				1					Yes	Yes	"	Meath	
				1					No	No	"	Tipp	
1									Yes	Yes	P.	Aberdeen	
									"	"		Midd	
				1					"	"	R.C.	Leitrim	
				1					"	"		"	
				1					"	"			
									"	"	P.	Norfolk	
				1					"	"	R.C.	Wexford	
1									"	"	P.	Dorchester	
1									"	"			
				1					"	"	R.C.	Tipp	
				1					"	"			
				1					"	"			
			1										Plans Eng. 10/10/38
									"	"	P.	Norfolk	
									"	"		Glamorgan	
									No	No		Leicester	
									Yes	Yes		"	
									"	"		"	
									"	"		"	
									"	"		Perth	
1									"	"		"	
1									"	"		"	
	1								"	"		"	
	1								"	"		"	
	1								"	"		Cornwall	

348 ————————)

General

			Adults		Children		Infants		
			Male	Female	Boys	Girls	Male	Female	Male	Female	
2nd Class				1	2			1			
Assisted 2nd Class					2						
Steerage		6	6	78	2	6	1	2	3		
Free				10	33						
Remittance		11	11	29	27	22	19	3	1		
On Ship's Articles				1							
Indented				7							
Bounty		24	24	151	12	14	15	2	2		
		41	42	215	76	42	36	7	8		
Births										2	
Deaths		41	42	215	76	44	36	7	7		
		41	41	214	76	42	36	7	7		

SS *Waroonga* ship's manifest (May 1885)

Summary

													Males	Females	Souls	Statute Adults
1	1												2	2	4	3½
2														2	2	2
15			11	6	5								29	12	21	32½
24			15										10	33	43	43
58	33	3	10	8	1								65	57	122	98½
1													1		1	1
7													7		7	7
66	11	1	65	9	1								191	53	244	225½
194	43	4	109	23	5								305	159	464	413
					2									2	2	
194	43	4	109	23	7								305	161	466	413
1			1										1	1	2	2
193	43	4	108	23	7								304	160	464	411

Chapter 7: Charlotte and George – 1887

Frederick Thomas Horsfall found it impossible to keep his opinions to himself. He repeatedly told any other lighterman unlucky enough to be within earshot how disgusted he was with the behaviour of a few of their colleagues. Although nine years had passed since the *Princess Alice* disaster, Frederick was still as passionate and still as disappointed in his fellow rivermen as ever. Although many lightermen felt as he did, he was more vocal than most, and this did nothing to endear him to the other men working the Blackwall docks. Especially those who were found guilty of fighting over the floating corpses, many had been brought up on charges before the Waterman and Lighterman guild and had been fined or suspended and wished only to have the whole episode forgotten.

Edward Bignall had known Frederick all his life. Frederick's father had worked for Edward's father until his death. Old William Bignall had been at the celebration to welcome baby Frederick into the world. They respected each other and were as close to being friends as dock protocol allowed. Edward was keen to show his support for Frederick and proposed putting him forward to represent the company in the Thomas Dogget's Coat and Badge rowing race. This was the oldest annually contested race in the British sporting calendar. It had been run on the first weekend of August since 1715 over a course of four and a half miles between The Old Swan Tavern at London Bridge and The Swan Tavern at Chelsea. Blackwall docks had not won the race for seventeen years. Edward Bignall suggested Frederick's name was put before the Fishmongers Company race committee, who organised the event. Normally he would not have qualified as it was meant for men in their first years of freedom, and he was now fifteen years out of apprenticeship. Edward put a compelling case for his man, citing his dedication to the river and his family's long service and sacrifice going back three generations. Now they would have to wait for a decision, only time would tell if he was accepted. Regardless of the outcome, Lighterman Horsfall was honoured to be chosen to represent Blackwall.

Life at home was busier than ever for Frederick. Charlotte had now borne eight children, ranging from her namesake Charlotte, at fourteen years old, to young George, not yet six months old. George was a sickly boy; he had suffered breathing difficulties from the day he came into the world. Charlotte and Florence, the older daughters, took turns in nursing him. Charlotte, his mother, had given birth many times, but after George she felt weaker, the birth had taken more out of her, and she was taking much longer to recover. Maybe it was her age, she was now thirty-nine, maybe it was the effort of caring for five children under five years old at the same time as recovering from childbirth, she was always tired. Three of the children, Florence, Frederick, and Margaret, were now at school. Margaret had started after Christmas; she was now five. Charlotte, the eldest child, had left school at fourteen to go out to work, which meant Florence was often kept at home to care for her younger siblings when her mother was not well enough to look after them. Recently that had been all the time. Florrie was worried about her mother. Lately she had hardly been strong enough to give her instructions; she wanted Florrie to concentrate on looking after the others. She would say, "Leave me be, pet, sort out that boy, he's coughing agin."

"But, Ma, you need food too. Let me warm some broth for you?" At eleven years old, Florence spent her days washing, cooking, and feeding their family, not to mention nursing George and her mother during the day. When her sister Charlotte came home from work in the evening, she took over caring for the baby.

One constant was the daily reading session, Frederick never missed it, with the younger ones sitting round the old table with the paraffin lamp and the newspaper. Florence was too busy with her chores to get involved, but she knew when it was nearly ended, and she always stood behind her father. "Go on, Pa, tell 'em," she would say, grinning and remembering being three years old again as if it was yesterday.

The others would all echo in unison, "Come on, Pa, say it, say it."

"Well, you know when I says it, yer little ones all gotta be off to bed?"

"I know," says Florence, winking at her father, "that's the best bit."

Frederick clears his throat, and with a profoundly serious expression and his deepest voice, he says, "Well now, nuff red, nuff sed, time fer yerz off to yer bed."

Bedtime always started the same, kisses for Ma and Pa and baby George, and a special hug for Florence, followed by a chase up the stairs and lots of screaming and laughter. "You gettin them kids excited agin 'fore bed, Frederick Thomas?" their mother would reprimand him, although he noticed lately, without any real enthusiasm for a fight anymore.

George had been snuggled up on his mother's lap, wrapped in a patchwork blanket Frederick's mother had knitted over thirty years ago when he was born; they had used it for all of their children. His wheezing was worse today than normal, and his mother noticed how hot he was. "The baby's burning up, Fred," she said when the four youngest had gone to bed but without opening her eyes. "I'm not happy 'bout him. If he's no better tomorrow, we'll call out the doctor."

When Frederick thought about it later, he blamed himself. Charlotte was tired, she just needed George to rest so she could sleep. She always believed she would feel better tomorrow, she would deal with him then. He trusted his wife's judgement, normally impeccable when the children were concerned. He should have taken control; he should have taken George to the doctor straight away. Florence was the first to realise there was something wrong. She normally got up during the night when she heard George coughing and went into her parents' room to pick him up and rock him back to sleep. When she woke up, she heard her father moving downstairs, but the rest of the house was quiet. The January morning was bitter cold; there was ice on the inside of the children's bedroom window, and it was still dark outside. Her sister Charlotte was fast asleep in the small bed they shared, as were the rest of the family. Florence picked up her cardigan and wrapped it around her shoulders. As she tip-toed across the bare floorboards, they creaked, each and every step she took created a noise of wood grating on wood. However silently she tried to move, her footsteps sounded like an old three-mast tea clipper swaying in the wind on its mooring in Wapping dock. She crept into her parents' room to check on George, he would need a clean cloth nappy by now, and he would also need feeding.

When the family moved in, the house had some pieces of furniture already there: two old beds and the old kitchen table that the family sat around to prepare and eat their meals and learn to read at. There was also an old chest of drawers in the parents' bedroom, which was made of mahogany and stood five feet tall; it had three large and two small drawers. Over time, one round foot had broken off and had been replaced with a square chunk of oak, the veneer on the top was peeling off and two of the drawer knobs were missing. All the family's clothes were kept in the three large drawers. The right-hand drawer held nappies and baby clothes, and the top left-hand drawer was kept as a crib for their newborn babies to sleep in. Over the last few years, it was in use constantly, no sooner had one baby outgrown it than another replaced it. It was lined with old newspapers with a towel laid over them and granny Sarah's knitted blanket used to cover the baby.

Florence crept in, trying not to disturb her mother, and picked up her brother. "Come on, treacle, let's get you cleaned up. Oh! Little un, yer freezing," she said as she cuddled him to her face. "George! George!" she raised her voice as she looked at his face. "Ma, there's something wrong with the baby." Florence was now panicking as she ran over to her mother's bed, holding George in her outstretched arms.

Frederick heard the commotion and reached the bedroom door as Charlotte came to. "What's going on? You'll wake the whole house, girl."

"It's the baby, Pa. He's not right, he's not moving, he's like a block of ice."

Frederick took his son and shook him. "Wake up, boy, please wake up."

In April 1887, three months after they lost baby George to bronchitis, Charlotte finally succumbed to pneumonia. Leaving a heartbroken husband with seven stunned children to care for.

Frederick had no choice but to withdraw his application from the Doggets Coat and Badge Race; his priority was the welfare of his family. He had no time for training and even less enthusiasm. He was replaced by a lighterman fresh out of apprenticeship. The race that year was won by a waterman from Richmond called William Giles-East. He later went on to become the champion sculler in England and was rewarded with an appointment as a Queen's Waterman. Frederick often wondered what would have happened had circumstances not conspired against him that year. He would certainly have been the oldest rower to have ever competed.

Chapter 8: To the Big Smoke – 1897

Ernest Walter Jennings was a confident, charming young man; he was medium height with narrow beady, hazel eyes and a mop of bushy brown hair. He was stout but working as a farm labourer had stopped him turning to fat, and despite his outside occupation his complexion was still fair. He always had a funny story to tell, sometimes they were even true. There were a dozen boys and girls around his age from the village, and he knew them well from their days at the small school. He was not academic, but he was always sharper than the others, cajoling and bullying them into his plots, convincing them everything would be all right. Some of the younger ones looked up to him as their leader; however, he had a cruel streak, and as a result, they were always wary. The girls were particularly aware of his temper because Ernest could be just as rough with them. He often tried to kiss or touch them, then got angry when they rejected his advances, grabbing them in a headlock or pushing them over before he stomped off home.

Great Bentley was an idyllic place to grow up. Ernest was never hungry, he had household chores like all the children in the village, but plenty of time for playing and exploring the woods and fields and ponds around his home. When he left school, he worked with his father, William, as a ratcatcher and farm labourer. His father was strict. When he gave Ernest a task, he expected it done or Ernest would not be paid, but he was always fair with him; he proudly told everyone that he had never struck any of his children. One day when Ernest got back from the weekly market in Ipswich, forty miles away, he realised he had lost the silver pocket watch his parents had given him on his twenty-first birthday. It was already getting dark, but his father sent him back out to search for it. "We need that cart in the morrow, boy, don't you dally. Be smart about it." His mother, Dianna, wrapped a honey sandwich in a cloth, and off he went. Ernest got home at two in the morning, cold, tired, and hungry. He had found it near the ford at Manningtree. He never mislaid it again. His mother spoilt him rotten as the youngest boy of seven. By that time, there was just him and his youngest sister, Grace, left at home. He quickly outgrew his small community and was desperate for a new challenge. The older siblings had moved away, and when they sent home letters telling of their adventures as soldiers or nurses, it stirred Ernest to dream of moving to London to experience the excitement the big city offered.

When he was twenty-two years old, he moved to London and lived with his brother Albert in Hammersmith, where he got a job as a porter at Charing Cross railway station. His real ambition was to follow Albert into the Metropolitan Police. He applied and was accepted in May the following year, 1898. His first posting was to R division in Plumstead in south London. He was so excited he felt his life was just about to properly start.

Life moved quickly for Ernest when he moved to Plumstead and found digs in a lodging house with six other men. All of them came from diverse backgrounds and had different jobs. George was a labourer who worked on the new tunnel going under the Thames at Blackwall. He was a local man. The others, like Ernest, came from all over the country, including two from Ireland and a Scot. He was the tallest man Ernest had ever seen. No one was sure quite how old he was, but he had a completely bald head with the bushiest red beard that filled his whole face, even growing out of his ears. They called him Muffs. George came from Farningham, a village three miles from their digs, he and Ernest became friends, and after a few weeks, George invited him to his family home for Sunday dinner. George's sisters Annie and Jessie, whose real name was Elizabeth, but no one could ever remember her being called that by anyone, looked after the house and their father after their mother had died when they were both young. Their father accepted they wanted to be more than his housekeepers. "Stop fussing over me, girls. Get out there and have some fun, will you? I can look after meself," he would say. However, neither of them was sent to school, and as Jessie was born deaf, Annie was her interpreter. Her father and brothers struggled to understand what she was trying to say, Annie just knew what Jessie was thinking; she was her link to the rest of the family, to the rest of Jessie's world.

Annie was a slight young woman, nimble and quick with a smile, laughing with her eyes. She was never still, like a bird, moving from one foot to the other. Her arms moved when she talked, a habit she got into that helped Jessie understand what was happening. She always looked to Jessie first, facing her and talking slowly so her sister could lip-read to follow the conversation. They laughed a lot together, especially when Jessie misunderstood what was said. Ernest was enamoured with Annie at first sight, her girlish sense of humour, the way she coped with them all, as his mother did. "More potatoes, Dad? George, did you get any cabbage? I did it special, I know it's your favourite," all while she organised her sister. "Jess, why don't you get the men more beer while I clear these plates." Annie was in her element, showing their new guest how well she ran the house. He was obviously enthralled by her. Each time she cast a furtive glance in his direction, she caught him staring at her.

She returned to the table with an apple pie that she had made that morning. She smoothed down her dress, wishing she had made more effort with her hair. Why had she not put on that other dress with the buttons down the front? It showed her figure off much better than this old thing she was wearing. "Well, Ernest, why don't you tell us all about your exciting job catching robbers?" Annie asked. Ernest checked she was not mocking him, but Annie seemed genuinely interested.

Ernest looked at her father, John, who nodded and smiled. "Why not, young man? I'm sure we'd all be interested." He had never seen his daughter this animated; she was glowing.

"Well," started Ernest, "I had not been on the job a six-month when I was walking my beat late one night down Bostall Hill when a man comes running up and tells to me that there's a light in the post office up there." Annie was mesmerized by his deep voice with his soft Essex accent, not quite the Norfolk drawl but much slower than she was accustomed to hearing. For once she ignored Jessie, who was struggling to lip-read as Ernest spoke in his unfamiliar accent, her father had already noticed. Ernest continued, "Me and this other fella, who had some sort of sleep problem, meaning he had to walk round at night before he nodded off, was a clockmaker, but I don't think that's why he didn't sleep. Well, anywise, we goes over to the post office, and I shine my bullseye lamp through the glass door, when I sees this man in there with a candle, and he sees me and runs out the back. So, I goes round the back and chases him, and his cap falls off. Well, he legs it good, over fences and stuff, and I lose him. Then as I come round the front, the other man, the sleepy one, has got hold of another bloke with no boots, what has tried to leg it out the front but run into old sleepy, who's a big lump by the way."

John interrupted him, "We gonna get any pie this side o' Christmas, lass? Less you can't eat an' listen to the boy at the same time."

Annie jumped at the sound of her dad's voice; she had become oblivious to anyone else but Ernest in the room. "Course, Dad, just interested in what George's new friend was saying." Her cheeks flushed red. Jessie's grin stretched from ear to ear, and she had to turn her face away to hide her smirk when Annie scowled at her. Annie dished out the pie, giving her father a broken slice without much apple in it on purpose; they ate in silence for a minute.

Ernest wiped his mouth and continued his story. "Well, when I checked his pockets out, he's got this knife, still got putty off the window on it, and he had a jemmy bar and a candle, still soft from being lit up. So, I take him off to the station, and I give him to my sergeant to book in. Then about an hour later, this other sergeant comes in with the herbert I chased, the one with no cap, who got away, so I identified him too. Now, the best thing is, cos it was an offence against the crown, the trial gets to go in front of the Old Bailey. There are some in my station been there ten years and never had one at the Bailey."

Ernest was given one Sunday a fortnight off, he cycled to Farningham to visit Annie. They walked through the woods at the back of her house where Ernest told her the name of all the plants and birds they saw, and they sat by the pond, where they shared their dreams and secrets with each other. They held hands and kissed; they spent a lot of time kissing. Ernest had learnt from his experiences with the village girls back home to be gentle with her. At first, she refused his marriage proposal, saying it was too soon and anyway she could not possibly leave Jessie or her father. However, John knew she must eventually leave their small world; even a blind man could see how much she was in love with this young policeman. He had all the charm, all the chat, he had ambition that he could not satisfy staying around their sleepy village. Annie loved her birthplace, but she too wanted to experience more of this world. John and Jessie both wanted her to follow her dream; they could both see how happy she had been these last months. Eventually, after many tearful nights and much soul-searching, Jessie convinced her that she could look after their father on her own. Annie came to realise life would continue in Farningham without her. She finally accepted Ernest's proposal. They were married in the Eynsford Baptist chapel six months to the day after George first introduced them.

Shortly after their marriage, Ernest and Annie Jennings found new accommodation in Erith. It was a damp, two-roomed flat with one large bedroom and an even larger kitchen with an old square wooden table and two odd chairs. There was a black coal stove, which dual functioned as the fire and as their cooker, one battered armchair completed the sparse furnishings. Annie managed to travel the nine miles alone to visit her family most weeks. Ernest usually made the excuse of work commitments, but honestly, Annie preferred going on her own; it gave her a chance to see Jessie alone. To laugh with her again, to gossip about their new lives and responsibilities. About the new people Annie had met, her new home and her marriage, especially about the marriage; they laughed a lot about that. Jessie talked about their family and the villagers they both knew. Ernest did go with her in August. It was John's sixty-fourth birthday. Ernest had a reason to accompany Annie this time. The young married couple wanted to share their news with the whole Flewin family, Annie was delighted to be expecting their first baby. Jessie laughed and cried and hugged her, Ernest beamed with pride as John shook his hand. A girl was born the following February. They named her Anne, but she was always known as Queenie.

ERNEST JENNINGS (104 R.) Early on February 21st Bennett spoke to me—I went with him to look through the glass front door of the Bostall Hill Post Office—by the aid of my lamp I saw McPherson come from behind the counter—I saw his three-quarter face quite plain—he was wearing similar clothes and this cap—he made for the back door—I went round to the back garden—I saw the same kind of man running up the back garden—! ran after him—he got over the fence—I followed for a while; and lost him—he went into another garden—I went back to the post office and found White captured by somebody—he was without his boots—he made a statement to me—I took him to the station—I searched him in the post office—I found a *jemmy* a screw-driver, and knife in the lining of his coat, and at the station this candle in his left hand pocket, and 6 1/2 d. in bronze in his trousers pocket—I gave a description of the other man to Cole—I afterwards saw him brought in and heard him charged—he said. "'It is not me: I have come from Dartford, and

how could I be at Dartford and there too?"—he had a handkerchief round his head and no cap—I asked him where his cap was—he said, "sold it to a man on the road for 6 1/2 d.," and he showed me 6 1/2 d.—I went with Bennett and searched the garden—we found this cap beneath a tree within ten yards of where I lost sight of him—from the top of Wickham Lane to the post office is about three minutes' walk—Welling is twenty to twenty-five minutes' walk—Wickham Lane runs from Plumstead High Street into Welling—Dartford is six or seven miles from the post office.

The Old Bailey post office burglary transcript

Ernest Jennings' Metropolitan Police application form (1897)

Chapter 9: Florence gets Married – 1897

Tuesday, 16 February 1897. The heavens had opened before dawn, starting as a gentle drizzle, progressing to heavy rain; it was now coming down stair-rods. The rain was bouncing up from the pavement almost to their knees, washing the night's detritus away towards the river, soaking the hem of Florence's new cream dress on the way. Frederick Thomas Horsfall tried to keep his daughter as dry as possible with his old coat; however, it was a futile gesture, the rain was too heavy. The new shoes he had bought for her were already soaked through. She had inherited her grandmother Sarah's dressmaking skills and made her own wedding dress, but it was now splattered with mud. Charlotte had plaited her sister's hair this morning and tied it up with strips of silk to match her dress, but parts of it had already come loose. To be fair, it had looked neater for longer than Charlotte had expected. The small wedding party huddled in the doorway of the West Ham Registry Office, shaking the water from their clothes. Her father, her sister, her best friend Alice Bick from the dressmakers where she worked, and her husband, Charles Bick, and of course Florence herself. Despite the awful conditions, Florence could not have been happier.

The wedding guests never thought this day would happen after she met that lad in the park twelve years ago. He was all she would talk about, think about, for months afterwards. She had only met him twice, and anyone who heard her talk would think they had been lifelong partners. Arthur said this, Arthur said that, Arthur was so funny, so kind, never a mention that this Arthur bloke left her here and went twelve thousand miles away. Many young men had tried to reach her over the years, a few even dared to ask her for a date; they were told plainly and sometimes not very politely where they could go. Recently, her family noticed the change. She had been like a schoolgirl these past weeks, dressing up to go out, disappearing for hours on end without explaining where she had been, even making the effort to tie her hair back neatly. Even so, they were shocked when Florence announced she was to get married in two weeks' time.

Her father met the groom for the first time on the night he proposed to Florence. He came to the tenement block where they lived to ask her father's permission. An unnecessary formality as she was no longer a minor; at twenty-two years old, she could marry him without her father's consent. Frederick was not yet sure whether he trusted this man, a little older than he was expecting at twenty-eight, but he seemed a decent man. They talked about his life, his job, his prospects, his family circumstances, which were not unlike theirs. A sibling and a parent had died in both families, with the heartache, pain, and upheaval that had caused to those remaining. He made them laugh when he related the experiences the family had in the early weeks of their life at sea. "But I never stopped thinking of yous, all of them years," he said as he brushed a wayward strand of hair from her face. Florence gazed into Arthur's face. She knew he was sincere.

Young Fred was only twenty when Arthur arrived in their home with tales of travel, ships and sailing the seven seas. He was suspicious of this gangly stranger with the weather-beaten face, burnt by the ocean sun and salt air. He had a black bushy moustache over a slightly crooked mouth, higher on the left, as though he had a broken jaw at some time, with black hair, oiled and combed back. He walked into their lives from nowhere and entranced his sister, who had been their surrogate mother for ten years. Why had he not been in touch with Florence for so long? Not even a letter to tell her he was on his way. Fred was protective of his sister in a way only twenty-year-old men find logical, only seeing the hurt Arthur had caused her for years, not ever taking Arthur's position into account. His pa had seen this protective reaction enough times to know when to calm the situation. It normally ended with his son punching someone extremely hard. "Why don't you tell us how it come about yer back in Blighty after so long, Arthur?" young Fred asked.

"I'll put some tea on if you're staying," offered Charlotte.

Arthur started his story at the middle, the most important part he needed to explain to them. "I did write yous, gave a letter 'bout two years ago to a mate I had below decks. He was a stoker like me; he left our ship, got a posting on a steamer coming 'ere from Newfoundland. I was heading back down to South America. I tell him to go to that address yous give me in Poplar. Not till I get 'ere a few weeks back I find out yous moved, I went there mesel when I first gets landed a few months back. Yous was me first port o' call, well, after I had a proper English beer down in Wapping o' course." He looked round the table with a guilty grin, Frederick and his daughter were smiling. Young Fred was not. Charlotte served the tea in their worn and tired heavy pottery mugs. Florence noticed her sister had given Arthur the best one with no chips and a handle; she smiled at her and touched her hand in a gesture of thanks.

Arthur continued, "Thought I were not going to see her no more, I was broken. I was just sitting on this wall outside yous old house when a woman comes out next door, reckon she was about a hundred. She wants to know what I's doing hanging about her wall, an' I tell her all bout yous, an the park bench, an' me, an' going to Australia an' everything. Then she tells me bout yous all, how yous lost yous missus, an' the little 'un a time back, Mr Horsfall. Then she tells how yous all had to move house on account o' that big dock strike back in '89, when yous had no money for a whole month. An' yous all had to live on what was given out by that charity, an' she knows where yous all gone, so that's how I come to find 'er again."

Florence could not help herself grinning like that Cheshire cat character. All those 'yous' she really would have to sort that out when they were married; she could definitely not have any children of hers speaking with that accent. She realised at this point he was not talking to her, he was talking to the rest of the family, seeking their approval. She was pleased he wanted them to accept him and like him as much as she did.

Over the next two hours, Arthur told them his story from the start, how his father Richard died only six months after emigrating to Queensland at sixty-one years old. He died content in the knowledge he had given his family the chance of a new and better life. He told them all about his family, about his mother, how she had coped with everything, how she still managed to laugh and make people laugh after all the traumas she had been through. How they had stayed in the small town of Nundah just North of Brisbane after his father died. Arthur never really settled there. His mother always blamed it on the young girl he met before he left London, said his mind was never straight after that. He found a job on a steamship as an engineer's labourer running between Brisbane in Queensland and Sydney in New South Wales. He made them all chuckle when he described being in the boiler room, with no space to swing a cat, in one hundred and ten-degrees Fahrenheit in just his pants, stoking the boilers, having to drink water from a Pani gallon bucket, in order to keep hydrated enough just to stay alive. After two years, Arthur described it 'as reaching the dizzy heights of third engineer'. This promotion allowed him to sign up for five years on a ship crossing the Pacific, trading up and down the American coast. He thought it would be heading for London, but it turned round and headed back to Adelaide. Eventually, he transferred to a London-bound ship from Rio de Janeiro, and here he was. Young Fred sat transfixed, the stories of life on board, the camaraderie, the ports Arthur had seen; he knew that was the life for him. He just had to find a career that did not involve stoking boilers. Florence, for her part, realised that if she did not nail down Arthur's boots very quickly, he could be off around the world again, and she would lose him for another twelve years. The first date available at the registry office was two weeks' time; the wedding must be on Tuesday the sixteenth.

Chapter 10: Limehouse – 1906

Limehouse is an area of the East London docks that has been full of pubs, brothels, and gambling dens since the late 1880s. A copy of the Poverty Map of London in 1898 shows Limehouse as one of the areas of greatest poverty and describes it as 'filled with the lowest class, vicious and semi-criminal'. Into this squalid part of town, Chinese dockers came to live, those from Shanghai set up in Pennyfields, and those from Canton moved to Limehouse Causeway. They mainly worked for the East India Company; however, the accommodation the company provided them was so cramped most sought housing elsewhere. Many others had worked for the EIC and had been sacked from the ships that imported tea, silk, or opium. Opium had been freely available from chemists in London for twenty years, sold as laudanum, literally translated as 'worthy of praise'. It was used for every ailment from bronchitis to sexual dysfunction and as a painkiller; some parents even gave it to their children as a sedative to help them sleep. One beneficial side effect was constipation, which was particularly helpful in the treatment of dysentery and diarrhoea; however, the drug proved to be highly addictive. There were not actually that many Chinese that stayed on in London, a couple of hundred by the turn of the century, as most returned east to their homelands. Those that did stay were predominantly men, as Chinese women were restricted by British law from immigrating. The problem with Chinese women being excluded from Britain was that the men then turned to English women for partners, which only added to the huge resentment felt among the locals, who were already fearful that Far Eastern dockers were taking their jobs. Since the Second Opium War finished in 1860 between China and Britain, there had been extreme prejudice towards the Chinese. The British press fuelled the situation, describing immigrant Chinese men as 'yellow peril' and exaggerating the number of English brides who actually married them; this stirred up even more hatred. Into this racially charged and desperately poverty ridden Limehouse arrived the newly promoted Sergeant Jennings from Dartford division.

On the new sergeant's beat, there were eleven opium dens. These were slum houses where curtains were hung to form room partitions, allowing clients to lay on beds and chairs in privacy. In China, opium houses were often grand, ornate buildings established for the pleasure of the wealthy, many of whom regarded opium smoking as a leisurely ritual equivalent to afternoon tea in English society. Originally, the Limehouse dens were set up as businesses to cater for European seamen who had become addicted while serving in Asia and India, but as they became more established, the clientele grew to include Londoners of all classes. Opium was smoked from pipes in small alcoves behind curtains and walls, and unlike gambling or drinking, this was a solitary addiction, where the user could spend hours or days in a stupor, safe from assault or robbery. Like the gambling houses, opium dens were illegal and only survived with the protection and cooperation of the local police force, who could, if they chose to, arrest the proprietors and close them down.

Ernest was a pragmatic man, and he had learnt in the eight years he had been a policeman that some establishments were better kept in plain sight rather than hidden underground. When he first got promoted, he was approached to join the Freemasons. At first, he was dubious, but his old inspector at Dartford convinced him that he was better a member than an outsider. Looking around at the faces of his brothers at his first lodge meeting, he realised how far the local Freemasons' influence stretched and that joining had been a sound decision. Bolstered by his fellow brother Freemasons' support, his first task was to introduce himself to all the owners of the illicit drinking pubs and clubs, gambling houses and opium dens, along with all the brothel madams in Limehouse. He made it clear that he wanted no trouble on his beat and that he would not tolerate turf wars to gain next door's custom, and that he would not allow anyone else to interfere with their business as long as everyone cooperated. He hoped this would keep his streets quiet. He also made it clear that if those running businesses in this part of London did not like his terms, he would follow the letter of the law and they would not be trading much longer.

Sergeant Jennings, his wife Annie, and their daughter Queenie, now five years old, lived at the station house in Limehouse. It was a two-bedroom flat on the top floor of the police station, with running water inside and a toilet just for their use, and it was comfortably furnished without being grand. Considering the abject poverty in the surrounding area, the Jennings family lived in luxury. Ernest earnt a good wage, even without the sovereign a month he collected from 'his friendly businesses', his accommodation and uniform was included, and the job was secure, unlike the majority of the inhabitants of Limehouse. Working in the docks had always been tough, physically and economically. However, in the last ten years, with the influx of foreign labour, particularly from Africa and Asia, dock work was scarce for many. Men who had worked as stevedores for years took jobs as ship's crew, often away from their families for weeks and months on end.

Annie met one docker's wife while she was in the local corner shop, whose husband had resorted to being a seaman. Annie was waiting to be served, and the lady was in front with three small children. She was tall, at least six inches taller than Annie, but well beyond slim; she was skeletal. Her wrists were tiny; they reminded Annie of a pigeon's leg, the bone protruding like a bird's kneecap. Her face was gaunt, every miniscule shape of the cheekbones could be seen, and her hair was dull and lacklustre. As Annie glanced down, her legs were no thicker than her wrists. She was pleading with the Jewish shopkeeper, who although sympathetic, was firm in his decision not to allow her any more credit. "I already tell'd yer, Mr Goldie, my John gone got his self a job on a boat, right enough, gonna be home any day now an' I'll be good fer it."

"It is Goldstein, Mrs Tullet, how many more times, Goldstein, not Goldie. You told me you'd settle last week and the week before already, enough is enough. No more credit until you pay your dues." The shopkeeper had seen it all before, half the families in Limehouse were in the same position.

"I got free kids an' yer tellin me yer won't give me no grub?"

"I told you, Mrs Tullet, as soon as you pay up, I will be happy to serve you again, but I got a business to run."

"We's hungry, Ma," said the small girl, a miniature copy of her mother, Annie guessed she was maybe three years old from the size of her. She was actually six, tiny, and malnourished, with a worn and dirty dress, and Annie noticed she had no shoes at all.

Mrs Tullet spun round. "Come on, kids, let this shyster be."

Annie Jennings was not sure why she left the shop and followed the family outside, but she did. "Excuse me, Mrs Tullet, I heard you talking in there. Have you got a minute?"

The distressed group stopped and looked at her. "Yer that rozzer's missus, ain't yer?"

"I am Sergeant Jennings' wife, yes, how did you know?" asked Annie.

"He was the one what give my Charlie a clump round 'is 'ed last week, outside the baker shop, lost 'is 'earing for a week 'e did, didn't yer?" The boy nodded on cue, rubbing his left ear.

"That sounds like my Ernest. What did your lad do to deserve that?" asked Annie.

"Nuffink, my boy done nuffink, he was just 'aving a small dried-up crust away, weren't even for 'im, it was fer his sisters, like I say, nuffink. Your old man then collars 'im an gives 'im a cuffin."

Annie suppressed a smile. "When did your children last eat, Mrs Tullet? When did you last have food? I can see you are not eating right."

"Eating right, yer 'aving a chuffin larf, missus? I got no dough, missus la-de-da, what is we s'pose to do till my John gets 'ome? Get food out 'o thin air?" She grabbed the smallest child by the hand and started to walk away.

"Mrs Tullet, stop. Please, let me help." Annie Jennings returned to the shop and paid a stunned Mr Goldstein the outstanding Tullet tab. She bought a loaf, butter and some jam; the total cost was less than she would have spent for her and Ernest and little Queenie's tea. She hoped Mrs Tullet would be grateful, she probably was, but she had never had a stranger help her before, and her suspicion was overriding.

"I ain't got no money to repay yer, yer know that? Not till my John gets 'ome." Annie carried the shopping back to Doreen Tullet's tenement block and they talked on the way. Although their social circumstances were vastly different, both women had similar aims and ambitions; they merely wanted to bring up their children, care for their husbands and survive life in one of the most inhospitable areas of London. Doreen told Annie that her husband was on a ship heading to Marseille. She said she had gone into Florrie Spiers's flat next door because she could read and had one of those world map books. Florrie had shown Doreen where her husband was sailing to, down to Africa, then past Gibraltar and up past Spain. He was due home last month but had still not returned yet.

When Annie got home, she told Ernest who she had met, and the awful state the family were in, how hungry they were, unable to feed themselves until her husband returned from sea. "Well, you keep away from the Tillett family, you hear me? They're bad news," he told her.

"Tillett, no Doreen Tullet was the woman I met."

Ernest laughed. "Well, you must have met her at the Jew boy's shop, yes? She never calls the Jew by his right name, so he won't use her proper name either. Been going on for years by all accounts. She's the wife of John Tillett. He was involved with that other Tillet who rallied the dockers out on strike. You remember the Great Dock Strike fifteen-odd years ago? Well, they got the workers the tanner a day they called for alright, but it cost the employers a fortune. Apparently, he can't get a job round here for love nor money. He's working the ships now."

Annie went to bed that night with Ernest's words ringing in her head. She lay awake staring at the dull glow of the moon shining through the gap in the curtains, imagining walking in Mrs Tillett's shoes. How could she ever sleep knowing that family's plight? She pictured them huddled in their bare room, hungry and cold. Doreen had told her earlier how she had already pawned everything they could and sold any of their clothes and blankets they could spare; that was why her daughter had no shoes. That family literally only had each other to keep them warm.

If her husband did not return soon, they would be in the workhouse. That night in bed, Annie made a decision.

The following morning when she visited the shop of Mr Goldstein for her shopping, she bought an extra loaf of bread, butter, some suet, carrots, greens, and potatoes, enough so Mrs Tillett could make a broth. She also took a small spare blanket, rolled it inside her coat and paid a visit to the tenement block. Doreen and her children were sworn to secrecy. Annie knew if Ernest found out, there would be hell to pay. He made it quite clear she was not to get involved, but she figured his wrath was nothing compared with how she would feel herself if she did nothing to help the beleaguered family. This continued for two more weeks. Until one day, Annie met Doreen in the corner shop. "Hello, Doreen. How are you all doing, sweetie? I haven't seen you in here in a while."

"Mrs Jennings, yer never guess, the best news ever, my John come home last night, we was all chuffed to bits to see 'im, right enough. I told him all about yer, an what yer done fer us since he be gone." She beamed, holding Annie's hand between her bony fingers.

Annie flushed, then muttered something like, "It was nothing really, please, you're very welcome. Sorry, I've got to go." She turned and left the shop quickly, forgetting the food she went in for. Everyone in the shop had heard their conversation. What if news of her charity got back to her husband? She did not realise that the Jewish shopkeeper had known since that first day what she was doing. No one with only one child buys that much food every day for a fortnight.

"Mummy, what is a 'backhander'?" Queenie asked her mother.

"A backhander? Where did you hear a thing like that, sweetie?"

"Me and Lucy Tillett was out playing hopscotch in the street with little May Spiers from next door to where Lucy lives, an 'er two brothers was there. An' the bigger one, Arthur, says that my dad takes backhanders an' is bent, an' he don't wanna play with me," she answered.

Her mother was left speechless. "And what did you girls say back to those boys, Queenie?"

"Well, Lucy tells them that all bobbies are bent, an' it's got nothing to do with me. An she won't have nothing said against our family, an' if they don't leave us be, her brother will do 'im, an Arthur says let him try," says Queenie waving her arms descriptively.

"Best say nothing to your father, you know he doesn't like you playing with the kids from the tenement blocks. Now come in and have some tea, sweetie."

Queenie was a feisty girl, she had dark curly hair and pale skin, which gave her a doll-like appearance, and she had an answer for everything and everybody, like her father she was always more resilient than the other kids. Ernest thought she would have faced down a gang of pickpockets and dare them to try their luck with her. She had a stance that both amused her parents and infuriated them in equal measure, standing with her hands clenched into fists, on her hips, chin out, defying the world to cross her at their peril.

The following day, Annie dropped her daughter off at the Thomas Street Girls school, and she was on her way to the meat stall. She did most of her shopping at Mr Goldstein's corner shop, but on account of him being kosher, he did not sell pork, and Ernest did love a bit of bacon. Annie was walking down Narrow Street, past The Grapes pub, when a small man on the opposite side of the road caught her attention. He was walking purposefully towards Annie, looking straight at her. She became nervous. She did not think anyone would accost Sergeant Jennings's wife in broad daylight, but in these uncertain days, who knew. The distressed man crossed the road and stood in front of her. "You Mrs Jennings?" he asked. He had a surprisingly deep voice, considering his slight frame. His question was not menacing; however, something about the fellow made Annie feel uneasy. He was muscular, used to physical work, maybe forty-five years old, she guessed. He was dressed plainly, his clothes were clean but shabby, like many of the locals, but he somehow seemed out of place. His face was weather-beaten, and for the first time Annie noticed he had kind eyes, which nervously flitted about, taking in the activity in the street, watching every face moving left and right.

"Who are you, what do you want? I have to go, sorry," she muttered.

"Please, Mrs Jennings, just a mo, I need to talk to yer. My name's John Tillett."

Annie was flustered. "Not here, Mr Tillett. I'll meet you at the church up the road." And she hurried away with her head down.

John Tillett was confused, he was not expecting that reaction. He stood on the pavement for a few moments before following Annie, slowly at a distance to St. Anne's church. He started up the imposing steps, looking up to the clock mounted on the Corinthian columns, seeming to rise to the sky. He pushed open the large door, he had not been in a church for twenty years. John had forgotten what a cool, serene place a church could be. He saw Annie standing at the front pew facing the spectacular stained-glass window depicting the crucifixion; the sun was bright and cast the whole space in blue light. He headed down the long nave, feeling awkward and out of place, unsure of the reception he would get at the end.

As he reached Annie, she turned to face him, and they both blurted their apologies out to each other together. She continued, "I am sorry, Mr Tillett, did Doreen not tell you Sergeant Jennings don't know about your family? I need to keep it like that."

John smiled. "She told me exactly how it is, Mrs Jennings, which is why I never come to you at the station." He paused; he seemed nervous, he seemed to be in two minds as to what to say next. Annie said nothing, waiting for him to continue. When he spoke, his voice choked, he cleared his throat, obviously emotional. When he finally started talking, he could not stop, intent on telling her everything on his mind before she interrupted him. "Nobody never done nuffink fer us before. My Doreen tell'd me what you done fer us when I was gone working. Without yer there, Mrs, me kids would've been in the workhouse or dead. I'm never doing boat crewin' ag'in, I was s'pose to be back six weeks ago. It nearly killed me knowin' they had no means while I were held up." Annie saw he had tears in his eyes; talking about his family's plight was breaking his heart. "Yer can't imagine me relief when I come 'ome an' see 'em all there safe, a bit skinnier granted, but not dead nor sick nor nuffink. Yer really can't begin to imagine how I was. An' when she tells me bout yer, I nearly cried. Why? I said, why she do it? An' me Doreen says, it was just cause you're a good woman. An she tells me bout yer old man not happy with it, an all."

Annie started to explain, but he put his hand up, "Please, Mrs J, let me 'ave me say. I can never repay yer, whatever I do, however long God decides I do live, but we wanna make it up to yer a bit, to say ta, an all." John Tillett held out his hand, opened the palm and revealed a ring of twisted gold with three diamonds set in it. "It was me ma's, but she's gone. I went an' got it out the pawn shop down Pennyfields today. Me an' my Doreen decided we want yer to 'ave it, an' my ma would want yer to 'ave it. It ain't much to thank you fer the lives o' me family, but it's all we got in this whole world, barring our kids, o' course."

The ring Annie Jennings was given (1906)

Chapter 11: Frederick Leaves London – 1909

He sat on the wooden bench in the canteen of the steamship, cupping a tin mug of steaming tea between his gnarled hands. The SS *St. Louis* had rounded the Isle of Wight and was heading down to Cherbourg before continuing across the Atlantic. In eight days' time, they would dock in New York. By the end of April, he would be reunited with his son Harry and his daughters Rose and Esther. He had not seen the girls in fifteen years. He had written to them every single week, however that just made him miss them more. Every day he regretted sending them over four thousand miles away, across the Atlantic with his stepsister and her husband. Even though he knew they would be well cared for, that did not make him miss them less. There was a gentle drizzle in the air when they left Southampton but little wind, there had been a gentle drizzle in England for two months now, and that was definitely something he would not miss.

Life in London's docklands was hard, work was scarce, money was scarce, food was scarce, but people still looked out for each other and cared for each other's children. They shared what little they had with their neighbours and family. Frederick had found it both emotionally and financially hard when Charlotte died leaving him with seven children. He did the best he could, but he could not work as many hours as when he had a wife, which had affected his income. Florence had already been doing a lot of the household chores while her mother was ill; she looked after the younger ones, cooked, and cleaned, but he felt guilty that her childhood had been curtailed. The lady in the flat downstairs was a widow, she had two young children herself, and she was also called Charlotte, which just seemed fate to Frederick. They had talked to each other for years on the stairwell outside. Her oldest boy Henry was the same age as his Harry. Most of Frederick and Charlotte's initial conversations involved an apology, as the boys took an instant dislike to one another; one boy had said something or done something to the other. Frederick liked her. She was not like his old Charlotte, she ran a coffee house which was open six days a week, which meant her children were often looked after by neighbours or friends. His Charlotte had always insisted they looked after their children themselves, and when she became too ill to do it herself, her older children cared for her younger ones.

Charlotte Oliver's friendship with Frederick Horsfall had grown, they enjoyed spending time together. They were not juveniles, they had both had lovers before, and they missed the company. They decided to legitimise their relationship and married at their local parish church in West Ham in November 1892, with five of their children in attendance.

Sitting in the empty canteen on board ship with his tea, looking back at his life, Frederick acknowledged that was the biggest mistake of his life. Not only did Frederick's children not have a good relationship with his new wife's children, but they did not get on with her either. To make Frederick's life even more complicated, it was obvious that between work and her own children, she was not willing to spend time developing a relationship with his children. Her son Henry Oliver was seven when they married; he was a corpulent boy, not too clever, and less than popular at school, where he had very few friends. He was jealous of the Horsfall children and their social circle, their friends were always calling round to play in the street. As far as his mother was concerned, though, he could do no wrong. He bullied Frederick's youngest girls, Esther and Rose. The name-calling was constant, but when he stole their food, pulled their hair, and started touching them, life became intolerable for them. He made sure it was always when their brothers Fred or Harry were not around. He was not brave enough to face them, and he always denied it afterwards, saying the girls were making up stories to get him into trouble. The girls would tell their father when he came home, he initially made excuses for the boy, but eventually he started to see what was happening and how unhappy his girls were becoming. If he dared chastise the boy himself, Charlotte flew into a manic temper, throwing whatever was closest at Frederick and hurling the foulest abuse at him. Frederick's stepsister Mary always had a soft spot for Rose; they could have been sisters, except for the forty-year age gap. When she came to visit them and saw the situation for herself, she offered to take Esther and Rose to America with her. She had no children of her own to distract her, and Frederick knew they would be well cared for. Their stepmother did not object; two fewer mouths to feed and two fewer bodies occupying the little space they shared. Frederick did not realise at that time how much he would miss them.

Harry arrived in America by an altogether different route. In 1903 at the age of nineteen, Harry followed his brother into the navy. Fred had been a Royal Marine for five years by then and relayed exciting tales of his travels around the world every time he visited home. Fred loved his career and convinced Harry to follow him and join the navy. He did and signed on to serve for twelve years, but it soon became apparent that the life of a ship's stoker was not for him. Harry was transferred to HMS *Cumberland* in November 1904. A year later, while it was docked in New York, Harry was on shore leave when he met a seventeen-year-old girl called Christine Boyd. She had just arrived in America with her sister, Margaret from Scotland. They spent his forty-eight-hour leave exploring New York together. On 11 November 1905, Harry Thomas Horsfall left New York. However, instead of returning to his ship to complete the remaining ten years promised to His Majesty's service, he and Christine went on the run on a west-bound train headed for St. Louis.

Frederick senior had mixed emotions at leaving England, he knew his marriage to Charlotte had been a mistake. Theirs was never a loving relationship, more a marriage of convenience, but he had spent seventeen years with her in reasonable contentment, and they had two more children together that he was also leaving behind. Frederick delayed emigrating for years while trying to convince his wife to go with him, she refused and eventually the pull of America, and his children there, was stronger than his love of Charlotte. She never forgave him for leaving his new family to rejoin his old one.

He was also leaving his older two daughters, Charlotte and Florence, who were both married with children of their own; he would have loved to take them to America with him to reunite the family. He was extremely fond of both of them and would miss them terribly. Sitting below decks that day, he had no idea if he would ever see any of them again.

On the flip side, he was heading towards a new future; it made him smile to think of a new career at fifty-eight years old. What would he do in St. Louis? It was the fourth largest city in America, behind New York, Philadelphia and Chicago, and they had the Missouri River and the mighty Mississippi, of course, but Frederick was hoping he could get a job away from being a riverman. Dock work was physically hard, his joints were riddled with arthritis from over forty years as a lighterman. He had lugged cargo in all weathers, though mainly the wet, cold, and damp of England, not to mention hauling on the huge rudder to steer the barge itself. Harry had been in St. Louis for four years and assured his father there was work available for him. Frederick would live with Harry, who had married Christine in June, till he found himself a job and could afford to live on his own.

Frederick stood on deck with the other passengers in awe of the view as they steamed along the Hudson River into New York Harbour. Past the Statue of Liberty holding her flaming torch aloft, it was the symbol of freedom those on board had come here seeking. The statue had been in place for nearly twenty-five years, and the copper she was made from was just starting to discolour to a stunning verdigris. Frederick wondered what it would look like in another twenty-five years' time, no sign of the original copper colour at all. The SS *St. Louis* gradually came to a halt mid-stream, her engines were cut, and her anchors dropped. There was a general buzz about the deck. "Ladies and gentlemen, we will be staying here till they are ready for you at immigration on Ellis Island."

Another general buzz of disappointment went around. "How long for?" someone shouted.

"Long as it takes, chum," they were told. It turned out 'long as it takes' was two more days of frustrating, anti-climactic waiting, a ship loaded with eager passengers waiting to start their new lives.

By the time he had his medical checks and was processed through immigration, Frederick was desperate to be on his way to meet his family. St Louis was still a two-day train ride away, so he headed directly towards Pennsylvania Station. On the mile walk there, with his canvas bag over his shoulder carrying a life's possessions, Frederick saw things he had never seen in London. Skyscrapers were being built on every corner, dozens of them. He was used to the gaping holes while they were digging the London underground system, but the huge, towering buildings, how would the sunlight ever get down to the streets? When he arrived at the station, he was told there was no train until the following day, so he bought his rail ticket and found himself a diner. On his first night on US soil, Frederick Thomas Horsfall tried the American delicacy of grits, the first and only time he ever suffered the fate, and not for the first time, he wondered to himself if he had made a mistake moving here. Did all the food in this country taste as bad as that?

After a night's sleep on a bench in the station concourse, Frederick took his seat an hour before the train was due to depart. His seat next to the window gave him the perfect view as the train rumbled out of New York, across Pennsylvania, into Ohio, Indiana and on into Illinois; the landscape was like nothing he had ever seen before. Mountains, rivers twice as wide as the Thames and huge, seemingly endless fields of corn and wheat. When he arrived forty-eight hours later at Union Station in St. Louis, his son Harry was there to meet him. They greeted each other like long-lost lovers, with hugs and tears, both talking twenty to the dozen, so much to say, so many questions to ask. He met Esther and Rose and their new families the following week at Harry's house and had the emotional reunion they had all waited so long for.

Harry had trained as a Buick motor car mechanic when he arrived in St. Louis and had dreams of one day running his own dealership. He was working as a mobile mechanic, touring the state, carrying his tools in the sidecar of his chain-driven Harley Davidson motorcycle. Within six months of Frederick arriving in St. Louis, Harry was transferred to work in Cairo, a city one hundred and fifty miles away in South Illinois.

Frederick had still not managed to find a job that paid enough to live on, so Rose offered him a bed at their home. Rose was now twenty-six years old and had married an undertaker named Thomas Edmonds; he was a Scottish ex-pat, as was Christine, Harry's wife. The Edmonds family lived in St. Louis with their two children, ten-year-old Evelyn and an eight-year-old son named Ronald. Although he was grateful for their help, this was not the start to his new life that Frederick had envisaged.

Rose and Esther's ship's manifest (1894)

304959   304959   Chatham.

Name in full } Henry Thomas Horsfall

Date of Birth 6th January 1884.
Place of Birth Canning Town. London.
Occupation Laborer.

Date and Period of C. S. Engagements.	Age.	Height. Ft. in.	Hair.	Eyes.	Complexion.	Wounds, Scars, Marks, &c.
23rd September 1903 — 12 yrs	18.	5.7½	Bro	Blue	Fresh	

Ships, &c., served in.	List and No.		Rating.	Sub-ratings.			Badges.	Period of Service.		Character.	If Discharged, Whitl and for what Cause.
				Rating.	From	To		From	To		
Northumberland	14	456	Bts 2c					23 Sep 03	31 Dec 03	1903·12·03	
Acheron	"	"	"					1 Jan 04		1931·12·04	
	"	"	Sto.					8 Mchar	12 Apr 04		
Pembroke	S	3099	"					13 Apr 04	29 Nov 04		
Cumberland	S	143	"					30 Nov 04	11 Nov 05	V.S.	Run

Class for Conduct.

Clothing and Bedding Gratuities.		REMARKS.
£6.10. Ft.		Run 12 Nov 05. Cumberland. New York.
£3·10 28 June 04		

Harry's Navy certificate (1905)

LIST OR MANIFEST OF ALIEN PASSENGERS FOR THE UNITED

Required by the Regulations of the Secretary of Commerce and Labor of the United States, under Act of Congress approved February 20, 1907, to be delivered

S. S. _____ LOUIS _____ sailing from _____ SOUTHAMPTON _____ April 17, 1909

Frederick's ship's manifest (1909)

Chapter 12: Florence & Arthur William's Family – 1909

"Think that's enough, pet, don't yous?" Florence was exhausted. Arthur had to admit he had seen her looking more attractive. Her hair was plastered across her sweat-covered face. She was sitting up in their bed against the mahogany headboard, inlaid with yew in the shape of a Greek vase; they had bought it when they moved in from the family that had the house before them. The previous family had moved out to a one-roomed flat over a butcher's shop in Camberwell on account of the man's job being there. Florrie and Arthur knew them from the Barge House pub they drank in. Well, Arthur knew the husband to be exact. Florrie went in there once and did not like the smell, so avoided it after that. The pub was on the corner of their road, and Arthur had to negotiate his way past it on the way home from work. He failed most nights. Arthur was listening to the chap telling George, the landlord, about how that was all he could afford over on the south bank, but he needed the work so needs must. His wife and three children would have to manage, he had to be out as soon as. Arthur and landlord George had become good friends over the past few years. So, when the man told his story, Arthur thought he might be able to help them both out of their predicament. The next Saturday, Florence and Arthur had the house keys to number thirty-three Bargehouse Road, the rent book, and a new bed. The fact the pub was on the same road, even closer for Arthur, was an added bonus.

Florence was in bed cradling her two new babies. She knew she was expecting of course, but twins was a shock. "Bloomin' right that's enough. You keep away from me, yer 'ear me?" She laughed, it hurt. "Good news is we can use both names, yer chose a girl's name, I chose a boy's, one of each, eh!" If it was a girl, they talked about naming her after Florence's mother again,

Charlotte, but their first daughter, Jane Charlotte, lived less than a year, and Florrie was superstitious about re-naming a baby. Dorothy Lillian it was then, they would call her Doll though, and Harry George after Uncle Harold in America. This made five: Arthur Henry the eldest child, now eleven. Frederick Percy, two years younger. Then Little Ivy, such a sweet-looking girl, three years old, but she looked nearer two, and now the twins. It would have been seven with Jane Charlotte and if May Rose had survived. May really was a body blow to them all; she was nearly four, and they thought she had got over the riskiest age. That morning Arthur Henry woke first as always, lit a lamp to go downstairs and fill a bucket of water from the standpipe outside so the family could wash, that was always his job. He looked across to the mattress May was sleeping on; she was lying prone on her back, one arm pointing north, one pointing east, like nine o'clock, with her eyes open, staring at the ceiling. He would not forget the empty feeling he felt in the pit of his stomach. Arthur could recall the exact feeling he felt that morning throughout the rest of his life.

The grief he saw displayed by his parents exceeded anything he ever experienced before or after. His mother, normally the most thoughtful woman on earth, did not have a kind word or act for any friend or family who called to console her, and there were many. His father showed his pain in a separate way; he spoke to no one about his loss. He was an engineer rebuilding ship's steam engines, and he continued working, day after day, harder than ever and longer hours. Then, after work, he would call into George Crowe's pub and drink until closing time. He could not bear to go home and see the pain on Florrie's face. She attributed this time to the start of his serious drinking, he drank to drown his sorrows and forgot to stop when the pain had eased.

"Yous OK then, ducks? Think I'll pop down the road, wet the newbies' heads," her husband stated rather than asked.

"I shall be fine, sweetie. I got young Arthur if I need anything, ain't I, Art?"

Her son was standing in the doorway. "Course, Mum, anything yer need."

"He's a good lad, right enough," his dad said and rubbed the boy's hair as he hurried past.

Arthur Henry saw the look of disappointment in his mother's eyes, but she just threw an unconvincing smile at him and shrugged her shoulders, not willing to criticise his father. "Now come here, sweetie, and take the weight o' one o' these lumps off me, will yer?" The gangling boy rushed over to the bed, more than happy to be involved with the babies. As he sat on his dad's pillow, cradling young Harry, he wondered if the baby would remember this moment. He thought back to his childhood. Arthur's earliest memory was standing at the dockside, watching soldiers in bright red uniforms board a troop ship. His father told him later they were off to South Africa to fight the Boers. The last time a British army went to war wearing red uniforms. Baby Harry Spiers might not remember this moment, but he would feel the bond, feel the love of his older brother from the first day he was born for the rest of his life.

The following day, Sunday, 28 November 1909, Aunt Charlotte, Florrie's sister, came to their house. She was cuddling the babies and was staying for a few days to look after them and the new mother. Florence realised how much she missed her family now; she felt sad she was unable to share her new children with them. Her mother, who she barely remembered, and now her father, who had only emigrated earlier this year, he had always been there for her, and she already missed him terribly. She feared he would never meet his new grandchildren.

Arthur and his brother Fred were playing football in the street, Ivy was sitting on the doorstep with her doll, pretending to nurse it like she had seen her mother do. Out of number twenty-two came a very smartly dressed girl. "Ain't you the bent rozzer's kid? What you doin' down our way, then, girl?" Fred called out to her.

"My father's been made up, and we're transferring out west some place, an' he ain't bent. You say that again an' I'll do for yer."

She was fearsome. Fred imagined Boadicea had looked like Queenie Jennings when she was facing the Roman invaders.

"What yer doin' ere then, if you're s'pose to be on the other side of town?" he continued, unperturbed.

Queenie had grown into a pretty girl, still doll-like, but she had the build of her father, not tall, stocky, but not fat. Her mother, Annie, had brushed and tied her dark, wavy hair back neatly with a pink ribbon that exactly matched the flowers on her dress. She was ready for her visit to Sunday school this morning. Her inquisitive eyes were burning as bright as when Arthur had seen her last, the day she was playing with Lucy Tillett outside the tenement block where he had lived. She was standing legs astride, her hands on her hips, in the same stance she had back then; he could see she was not about to back down. "That's a pretty dress, Queenie. Where yer off to today then?" enquired Arthur.

The change of tack threw her for a moment; she dropped her arms, turned slightly sidewards, and squinted suspiciously at him over her shoulder. "What you after, Arthur Spiers? I ain't got no sweets," she said belligerently.

"Just saying it were a nice dress, that's all. What's yer problem? I wouldn't want nuffink what yer old man's paid for anywise," said Arthur, now defensive himself.

"Me 'n my friend Lucy Tillett are off to Sunday school, that's all," Queenie replied slightly conciliatorily. "An' me and Ma and Pa are going to live at Brentford, that's right over the other side o' London, that is, as soon as my pa gets his new station job sorted. An' anyway my ma says I'm gonna have a baby to play with soon an' all, like what you lot have."

"Little scroats ain't no great shakes," said Fred, "all they does is cry, an' then me mother forgets what she's cooking us when they does. Yer better off as you is, I reckon."

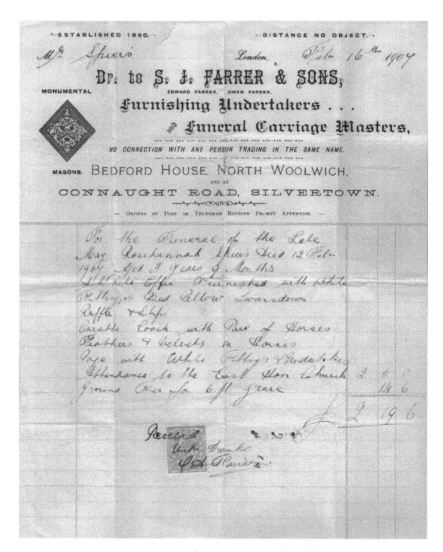

May Spiers funeral invoice (1907)

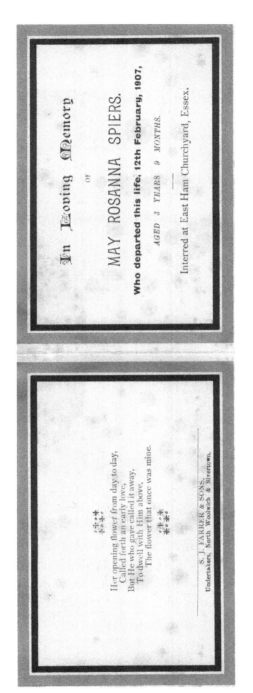

In Loving Memory

OF

MAY ROSANNA SPIERS.

Who departed this life, 12th February, 1907,

AGED 3 YEARS 9 MONTHS.

Interred at East Ham Churchyard, Essex.

Her opening flower from day to day,
Called forth an early love,
But He who gave called it away,
To dwell with Him above,
The flower that once was mine.

S. J. FARRER & SONS,
Undertakers, North Woolwich & Silvertown.

May Spiers remembrance card (1907)

Chapter 13: Frederick Thomas Horsfall and The Maltese Affair – 1909

Fred Thomas Horsfall was younger than Florence; he was only ten years old when his mother died. He had always been destined to follow his father and grandfather into the guild of lightermen until his father became disillusioned with the lighterman fraternity. He was in limbo for a few years, unsure of where his life was going, then Arthur Spiers appeared suddenly on the scene from Australia to woo his sister with tales of sailing the world's oceans. Fred knew from that day that is what he would spend his life doing. Obviously, the stories of stoking below decks held no appeal for him. Then one day, he met a man who he had known from around the docks a few years ago. They were in a pub in Blackwall, Bill was home on leave visiting his parents, he had just returned from his first tour abroad. He looked dashing to the young Fred in his crisp blue uniform. Fred was shy, but he managed to pluck up courage to talk to the man who told him his life story. It was amazingly full, considering he was not much older than Fred; he had done things, seen things that Fred could only have dreamed of. He told stories of the world with the same passion that Arthur had. The soldier explained why he left the humdrum physical life of a stevedore to achieve his ambition to see the world, and that is why he had joined the Royal Marines. Fred realised this man's story was his own. The day after the pub meeting, Frederick Thomas Horsfall travelled to Woolwich and applied to join up. He had been interviewed, undergone a medical and been accepted, all within six months. He was now a Royal Marine Light Infantryman. He had committed the next twelve years of his life to his Queen and Country.

After Private Horsfall's eighteen months' training at Chatham in Kent, he embarked on HMS *Warspite* in 1899, which was the flagship of the Pacific fleet, on a two-and-a-half-year tour of the

USA, South America and Canada. The tours were euphemistically called the Winter Tour, the Summer Tour, and the Tour of BC (British Columbia). While on ship away from home for all this time, Fred wrote a journal. He included training schedules, firing elevations and the bullet penetration of an entire range of materials along with the compass points. He also included songs and poems that the crew sang on board. At the beginning of December 1899, Frederick was transferred to the HMS *Leander*, where he spent five months. The revolution in Columbia had spread to Panama, and the *Leander* was packed with Royal Marines whose role was to protect the British and foreign nationals caught up in the conflict area. His first chance to try out his training. At the end of the civil disturbances in May 1900, he re-embarked onto HMS *Warspite* to continue its Pacific tour.

Fred was now twenty-three years of age, but he looked nearer seventeen. He was five foot six, baby-faced with a tanned complexion, he had short brown hair kept uniformly trimmed by the ship's barber. He had grey eyes that smiled on their own; they gave him the cheeky chappie look that girls found hard to resist. He was not altogether happy with his boyish looks, though, so he had both his forearms tattooed in the hope it would make him look more mature, one with a ship and the other with an anchor. He was trying to grow a moustache, but it was taking longer than he hoped, much to the amusement of his fellow marines.

On his return from the Pacific station, Fred Horsfall spent the next few months based at Chatham before joining HMS *Triumph* in 1908 as part of the Mediterranean fleet. His first port of call was Valetta in Malta. While on his first shore leave, he walked past a gallery selling oil paintings, he was looking for a gift for his sister Florence. He tried to find something interesting for her on each visit home. The first gift he had found in Chile in 1902 were two stuffed cobras mounted on wooded plinths, which her boys had found incredible. Doll hated them, they scared her to death, but Harry and Fred had a morbid fascination with them. "May we be helping you, please, no?" Frederick spun round, the voice was soft, quiet, and educated. He was faced by an olive-skinned beauty; she had dark hooded eyes under full, arched eyebrows.

She wore a white cotton blouse buttoned at the neck and wrists, along with a pleated, flowing green woollen skirt and brown leather boots buttoned to the ankle. Her thick, jet-black hair reminded him of Florrie's, much darker, of course, but the same thick, wayward mane; he wondered if she ever really tamed it either.

She smiled at him, and he realised he was just standing gazing at her, and he had not answered, "Oh! I am sorry. I, I, I mean, yes, yes, I do want to buy something." She cast her eyes downwards in a shy, embarrassed way, her enigmatic smile stretched to a grin. Fred stood in the small shop, in his shore-leave uniform, feet thirty inches apart in the regulation pose, shoulders back, fingers interlaced behind his back, holding his cap; he was struck dumb.

"Maria? Maria?" The awkward silence was broken by the entrance of an elderly woman from a door behind the counter; she was dressed from head to toe in black and had the same thick and unruly hair and hooded eyes as the young lady. She screeched something incomprehensible at the girl. Fred could not speak a word of Maltese; he had learnt some Spanish and a little Portuguese while in South America, but Maltese was altogether different. He could tell by the tone it was a furious rebuke. Maria glanced at Fred, then reverted her gaze towards the floor and hurried out through the door to the back room. Fred gave the old lady a curt bow, replaced his cap, and hurried out of the store.

The next day, all he could think about was Maria. Schoolboy error, he mentioned the girl to his friend, and within minutes his fellow platoon members were ribbing him mercilessly, "Horsey is in love, Horsey can't sleep he's smitten, come on, Horsey, give me a hug, pretend I'm your girl." He smiled, embarrassed at them because they were right. He had to see her again and soon.

The following day, Fred went back to the street where the gallery was situated and stood on the corner. He was trying to pluck up the courage to go in when he saw the old lady shuffle out of the shop, her head wrapped in a black scarf, bowed down against the chilly breeze coming off the sea. That was all the courage he needed; he charged headlong into the shop, grinning like an expectant schoolboy, only to be met by a seasoned sailor from his own ship. "Morn, Fred, what's you up to in 'ere, then?"

Fred stuttered, he seemed to stutter each time he came into this place, "I, I, I, was looking for something for my sis in Blighty, thought I would get her a picture."

"Me too."

At that moment, Maria came in from the back with a picture wrapped with brown paper and string. She hesitated when she saw Fred. The British tar took the parcel, nodded his thanks, and left. Maria was embarrassed, she started to say something then stopped. She alternated between looking at Fred, the door, and the floor. Instinctively, Fred glanced at the door, "My older mother has go out and buy food, she will be return soon," Maria said apologetically.

"Sorry, I wanted to see you again. Will you come for a drink with me out of here?" he blurted out. As he said the words, they seemed funny, and they both smiled.

"I cannot, I forbidden to meet with a man not from my country, especially not an English sailor man."

"Your grandmother?" he asked.

"She say sailors will not love me long, then I will not find a nice man who will marry me." Maria was now looking directly into his eyes, her eyes pleading for him to understand her predicament.

Fred was crestfallen, "Am I allowed to visit you in here, please, Maria?" She nodded. Fred visited every day, he waited until her grandmother left and used the excuse of choosing a painting if she returned unexpectedly.

Fred began bringing Maria small espresso coffees in from Caffe Cordina down the road. He then discovered their speciality, a honey ring filled with treacle and a tangerine sauce called Gaghaq ta' l-ghasel. Fred began buying an extra treat for her grandmother, which helped soften her heart when she caught him yet again in her shop. She grew to like him, and although she always pretended not to speak any English, they communicated very well, especially when he found a new sweet from the café for her to try, maybe a Sinizza, a puff pastry filled with ricotta.

Maria did start to wonder if he was actually visiting her or her grandmother. The old lady pretended not to understand his indecision, and she teased him, it was only a painting for his sister, after all, she chose to ignore his motives. Three visits to buy one picture, another four to buy the second. Sixteen visits in all; eventually, he bought four portraits, all by Arturo Petrocelli, an Italian artist specializing in painting character portraits. Two of the oils Fred bought were wizened old ladies, two were gnarled old men, the one with the aged man smoking a clay pipe was his favourite.

These visits were punctuated by enforced navy tours around the Mediterranean for Private Horsfall, away from Malta, and it was now three years since their first meeting. It was Christmas when Fred visited the shop; unlike his previous visits, he made sure the grandmother was in. He called into the Caffe Cordina on the way to pick up three coffees and three honey rings, and while they were seated in the back room of the shop drinking their coffees, Frederick knelt on one knee in front of grandmother and said in very broken Maltese, "Nista' jekk joghgbok nizzewweg lin-neputija tieghek?" He had tried over and over to memorise it but had finally admitted failure and written it on a piece of paper to read out.

Maria's grandmother grinned her best gap-toothed grin; he was not sure if she was happy at his proposal to her ward or amused by his attempt at speaking Maltese. She took his hand and kissed it; Fred took this to mean yes. He turned to Maria, still on one knee and from his tunic breast pocket, he produced a small velvet box with a flourish, like a magician conjuring a rabbit out of thin air. He took her hand and placed the delicate gold ring with the small rose-cut diamond onto her finger, it was a size too big, but he could always have it altered. He kissed her hand as he stared into her dark, seductive eyes, he saw they were filling with tears, he also saw she was grinning like a Cheshire cat. She threw her arms round his neck and kissed him; the old lady murmured her disapproval. Maria and Fred ignored her as they kissed each other for the first time.

When he returned to his ship, HMS *Triumph*, he was euphoric. Fred had been celebrating his engagement with his marine troop around all the bars of Valetta for twenty-four hours straight. They were signed in as they embarked up the gangway and told to report to the mess room immediately. When they arrived there, the crew were told that the ship was being redeployed permanently back to Chatham in forty-eight hours' time. A huge cheer went up among his fellow Royal Marines, many who were married with children in England, many who had sweethearts or family there that they had not seen in many months. Fred was crestfallen. He had only been engaged a day, and they had hoped that he and Maria would be married before he returned, and they planned for her to live with him in Chatham when he returned to Blighty. All shore leave had been cancelled with immediate effect in order to prepare the ship for sailing, so he had no chance to explain or even say goodbye. Fred did manage to send a message to her via one of the quartermasters who was charged with procuring some last-minute supplies, and he received a reply by the same route.

They wrote to each other every week. Fred told Maria over and over how he regretted signing up for a further twelve years extension, of which he had only served a few months before he met her for the first time in her grandmother's shop. He told her he would have happily followed his brother Harry's example and gone absent without leave had he known before he boarded ship that day that he was being sent back to England without her. For her part, she pleaded with her grandmother to allow her to follow Fred to England. She was adamant she would not allow Maria to leave Malta before being married.

1912 saw the Royal Navy's preparations continue for the conflict in Europe that now seemed inevitable. Britain had developed a new revolutionary Dreadnought class of warship and by the start of 1914 had forty-five of these, compared to the twenty-six similar ships in the German fleet. This was mainly due to the government's 1889 Naval Defence Act, which stated Britain must have at least as many warships as the next two largest powers in the world combined, so construction was upscaled accordingly.

Germany, Austro-Hungary, and Italy were on the one side. France, siding with Serbia, Russia and ultimately Great Britain on the other. Circumstances made war seem inevitable. The Balkans had been a tinderbox for some time, finally igniting when Montenegro declared war on the Ottoman Empire. Bulgaria, Greece, and Serbia joined the Balkan League in support of them. Morocco had initially been invaded by France in 1907, but in 1912 Germany had opposed The Treaty of Fez, giving France control in the area. Britain's support of France deterred Germany from getting involved for the time being. Meanwhile Italy unexpectedly attacked Beirut in February as part of the Italo-Turkish war, which had started in November the previous year, killing over a hundred Ottoman sailors and civilians. Fearing the Ottoman Navy may attempt to blockade the Suez Canal, the Italian Navy took pre-emptive measures and sunk both the Turkish warships. Every country seemed intent on fighting someone.

After a tour on HMS *Victory* when the Royal Navy were mobilized in August 1914, Private Horsfall was assigned to HMS Calliope on 4ᵗʰ of May 1915 and finally embarked on the new ship after its completion at Chatham dockyard in June of that year. The *Calliope* joined the fourth light cruiser squadron as their flagship under the command of Commodore Charles Le Mesurier; they commenced duty patrolling the English Channel and the North Sea. They joined the Grand Fleet in May 1916 and steamed towards the Danish peninsular of Jutland after reports The German High Seas Fleet had left port at 2am on Wednesday May the 31st. Admiral Sir John Jellicoe was the Commander-in-Chief of the British fleet, and his aim was to stop the enemy from reaching the safety of the German port of Wilhelmshaven. Two German ships were spotted twelve hours later, and the Battle of Jutland commenced. Just before nightfall, Fred and the HMS *Calliope* engaged the German destroyers *Kaiser* and *Markgraf*. Fred was manning one of the six-inch forward gun emplacements, the *Calliope* loosed off several shells at both the German ships. It appeared initially that the British had the best of the skirmish; however, as the two German destroyers turned and were heading away from the battle, the *Kaiser* let fly with a volley from her broadside guns. One shell hit the forward gun turret of the HMS *Calliope*. Ten men were killed instantly. One being Private Frederick Thomas Horsfall RMLI.

At the end of the two-day battle, the Royal Navy had lost six thousand men, and the High Seas Fleet had lost two thousand five hundred sailors. However, the Royal Navy had control of the seas, the German fleet did not set sail again during the rest of the war. Despite it having heavier losses, most commentators considered it to be a British victory.

Arthur was particularly late home on the night of the third of June; the talk all day in the London docks had been of the great sea battle and the losses the Royal Navy had suffered. This continued in the Barge House pub after work, knowledgeable seafaring men suggesting what may have happened, what may have gone wrong, why the losses were so catastrophic. At that time, no one really knew for certain, full details were still to be released. All the Admiralty had announced was that many British ships had been lost. It named eleven of the ships sunk but finished by saying six were still unaccounted for. This left Londoners and all naval townships around the United Kingdom either grieving or waiting to hear if their loved ones were safe. No sailors involved in the Battle of Jutland were definitely safe at this time, and many friends and relatives did not know for certain which ship a sailor had been posted on.

When Arthur walked through the door, Florence was distraught. Fred had a twenty-four-hour leave last month and had used it to visit her. Fred was so excited about having the chance to finally put all those years of training into practice and face the enemy. He had only joined HMS *Calliope* last June, and she was sure he would not have been reassigned that quickly. Was his one of the ships unaccounted for? It was still unclear. Florrie threw her arms around her husband's neck and sobbed; Arthur could not remember her being so distraught since they had lost their little May. "Our Fred's dead, I know he is, I can feel it, his ship has sunk, it's one of them not known boats."

"Whoa, our kid, whoa up now. Yous don't know that his were one what definitely went down, do yous?" Arthur attempted to console her.

Florence ignored him and continued, "Me an' Charlotte an' our Fred was like twins. Yer know what I mean, all three of us was twins, all knowing what the others was thinking an' feeling. I feel it in me bones, Charlotte do too, we talked today, she knows it too." Florence slumped into the chair, head in hands and silently sobbed.

When the letter eventually arrived from the Admiralty, Florrie knew in her heart it would be delivered one day but hoped beyond hope she was wrong. She prayed for a letter from Fred, saying he was in a hospital somewhere remote, recovering well, see you all soon. The envelope she received had the cross on it, drawn in black ink by hand, addressed to Florence Spiers as his next of kin. She ripped the end open instead of using a knife as she always did to open her post, she read the letter inside, which gave the date and time of death of Private Frederick T. Horsfall and offering her condolences. It was signed by Commodore Le Mesurier. Florence had done her crying, now she just felt numb, the realisation that all her fears about her brother had come true. Florence wrote to Maria in Malta the same day, explaining how Fred had been killed and offering her condolences. Maria never replied.

A further two months passed, and Arthur thought his wife had come to terms with the terrible loss of her brother, then a parcel arrived with Fred's personal effects. Strangely to Arthur, the thing that affected Florence the most was seeing his Certificate of Service. It listed all his postings, all the ships he had served on, the dates he embarked, the dates he disembarked, ending with an entry on the thirty-first of May this year, the reason for disembarkation was listed as *killed-in-action*. Florence broke down again for the first time in two months. Arthur was confused. Also in the parcel was the leather powder pouch Frederick had been wearing on his Sam Browne belt across his chest when the German shell hit his gun position; it had been damaged after a piece of shrapnel had penetrated it. Arthur expected this, or the book with all of her brother's handwritten notes and songs, to have a more dramatic impact on Florence than the service record, but seeing *killed-in-action* written down on his service record was final; it was more than she could deal with.

Fred and Maria in Valetta (1907)

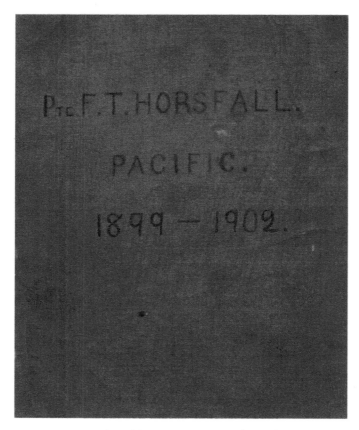

Frederick's marine journal (1899)

Log of H.M.S. Warspite. Flagship. I.H.P 8.000.. 8.400 ton.
Commissioned at Chatham for the Pacific Station
28th March.1899.

Left.	Date	Arrived at	Date	Miles	Country.
Chatham.	11.4.99.	Sheerness	11.4.99.	13	England.
Sheerness.	18.4.99.	Plymouth	20.4. "	282	"
Plymouth.	20.4.99.	Madeira	25.4. "	1.210.	Canary Islands
Madeira.	27.4.99.	St. Vincent	2.5. "	1.047.	Cape Verde Ilds
St. Vincent	4.5.99.	Monte Video	21.5. "	3.369.	Uraguay. S.A
Monte Video.	24.5.99.	Sandy Point	31.5. "	1.344.	Patagonia S.A.
Sandy Point	3.6.99	Sts of Magellan	5.6. "	.	" "
Sts of Magellan	4.6.99	Valparaiso	12.6. "	1.269.	Chili. S.A.
Valparaiso	16.6. "	Coquimbo	17.6. "	192.	" " "
Coquimbo.	3.7. "	Callao.	9.7. "	1.103.	Peru. "
Callao.	12.7. "	Paita.	15.7. "	576.	Columbia S.A.
Paita	15.7. "	Tabago Isle	20.7. .	766.	" "
Tabago Is	20.7. "	Calebra Bay	23.7. "	504.	Mexico N.A.
Calebra By	24.7. "	Acapulco.	29.7. "	907	Vancouver Is.
Acapulco	1.8. "	Esquimalt	14.8. "	2.530.	British Columbia
Esquimalt	29.8. "	Nanoose By	29.8. "	56.	Canada.
Nanoose Bay	30.8. "	Comox.	30.8.99.	71.	North America
Comox.	1.10. "	Departure By	1.10. "	40.	" "
Departure By	2.10. "	Esquimalt	2.10. "	105.	
Esquimalt	2.10. "				

Winter Cruize

Left.	Date.	Arrived.	Date.	Miles.	Country.
Esquimalt	15.12.99	Monterey	11.12.99	864	Canada U.S.A
Monterey	12.12. "	Magdalena B.	17.12. "	840.	Mexico N.A.
Magdalena B.	30.12. "	Acapulco.	4.1.00	826.	" "
Acapulco	6.1.00	San Jose	10.1.00.	560.	Guatemala C.
San Jose.	13.1. "	Panama	20.1. "	551.	Colombia C.A.
Panama.	23.1. "	Pt. Utria	25.1. "	237	" "
Pt. Utria.	25.1. "	Paytâ	30.1. "	523	Peru S.A
Paytâ.	30.1. "	Callao	2.2. "	576.	" "
Callao.	9.2. "	Coquimbo	16.2. "	1.103	Chili "
Coquimbo	23.2 "	Valdivia	26.2. "	630	" "
Valdivia	1.3. "	Telachuna	3.3. "	305	" "
Telachuna	4.3. "	Valpraiso	6.3. "	332	" "
Valparaiso	11.3. "	Coquimbo	12.3. "	192	" "
Coquimbo	30.3. "	Callao	5.4. "	1103	Peru "
Callao.	9.4. "	Acapulco	22.4 "	2.060	Mexico "
Acapulco	26.4. "	Monterey	6.5. "	1,813	U.S.A.
Monterey.	8.5. "	Esquimalt	12.5. "	864.	Canada
Esquimalt	29.5. "	Vancouver	30.6. "	85	"
Vancouver	8.6. "	Esquimalt	9.7. "	85	"

Cruise round the B. C. Islands. 1900

Left	Date	Arrived	Date	Miles	Country
Esquimalt	13. 7. 00	Barkley Sd.	14. 7. 00	106	
Barkley Sd	17. 7. "	Nootka	18. 7. "	130	
Nootka "	19. 7. "	Alert "	20 7. "	245	
Alert Bay	21. 7. "	Duncan .	21. 7. "	73 ¼	
Duncan . "	26. 7. "	Tribune "	27. 7. "	61.	British Columbia Canada.
Tribune . "	28. 7. "	Departure "	28. 7. "	37. ½	
Departure "	29. 7. "	English "	29. 7. "	36. ¼	
English "	30. 7. "	Vancouver	30. 7. "	.4.	
Vancouver	31. 7. "	Esquimalt	31. 7. "	82.	
Esquimalt	14. 8	Comox	15. 8.	145	
Comox	28. 9	Departure By	28. 9. "	40	
Departure Bay	29. 9	Esquimalt	29. 9. "	105	

Summer Cruise.

Left	Date	Arrived	Date	Miles	Country
Esquimalt	2. 3. 07	Honolulu	13. 3. 07	2,400	Hawaiian Isles
Honolulu	23. 3. "	Acapulco	11. 4. 01	3. 230	Mexico. N.A.
Acapulco	14. 4. "	San Jose	17. 4. "	600	Guatemala C.A
San Jose	22. 4. "	Acapulco	25. 4. "	600	Mexico N.A
Acapulco	27 4. "	San Diego	5. 5. "	1.426	U. S. A.
San Diego	8. 5. "	Esquimalt	13. 5. "	1.200	Vancouver
Esquimalt					Canada.

Island Cruise 1901.

Left	Date	Arrived at	Date	Miles	Country
Esquimalt	29.6.01	Vancouver	29.6.01	85	British Columbia
Vancouver	6.7. "	Comox	6.7. "	80	
Comox	8.7. "	Duncan Bay	8.7. "	60	
Duncan Bay	10.7. "	Beaver Hr	10.7. "	98	
Beaver Harb	12.7. "	Quatsino	14.7. "	80	
Quatsino	14.7. "	Esperanza	16.7. "	75.	
Esperanza	16.7. "	Barclay Sd	18.7. "	105.	
Barclay Sd	18.7. "	Esquimalt	19.7. "	142	

Homeward Bound.

Left	Date	Arrived at	Date	Miles	Country
Esquimalt	2.12.01	Monterey	7.12.01	8.10	U.S.A
Monterey	9.12. "	Acapulco	18.12. "	1.8.10	Mexico
Acapulco	20.12. "	San Jose	23.12. "	600	Guddemala
San Jose	2.1.02	Calebra Bay	4.1.02	370	Costa Rica
Calebra Bay	5.1. "	Bahia Honda	7.1. "	60	Columbia
Bahia Honda	8.1. "	Panama	9.1. "	220	Peru
Panama	11.1. "	Payta	15.1. "	850	Peru
Payta	17.1. "	Callao	20.1. "	520	Chili
Callao	27.1. "	Iquique	30.1. "	650	Chili
Iquique	3.2. "	Coquimbo	6.2. "	600.	Chili
Coquimbo	13.2.02	Valparaiso	14.2. "	190	
Valparaiso	19.2. "	Juan Fernandez	22.2. "	370	Chili
Juan Fernandez	22.2. "	Coquimbo	25.2. "	440	

Left	Date	Arrived at	Date	Miles	Country
Coquimbo	26.3.02	St of Magellan	1.4.02	—	Patagonia
St of Magellan	4.4. "	Sandy Point	5.4. "	—	"
Sandy Point	7.4. "	Monte Video	14.4. "	1.570	Uruguay
Monte Video	17.4. "	Bahia	25.4. "	1.344	Brazil
Bahia	28.4. "	St Vincent	8.5. "		Cape Verde Is
Cape Verde Is	10.5. "	Las Palmas	14.5. "	1.708	Canary Isles
Las Palmas	18.5. "	Madeira	20.5. "	474	" "
Madeira	23.5. "	Plymouth	28.5. "	270	England.
Plymouth	29.5. "	Sheerness	30.5. "	1176	"
Sheerness	11.6. "	Chatham	11.6. "	285.	"
				9	"

The summer, winter, and British Columbia tour schedule (1899–1902)

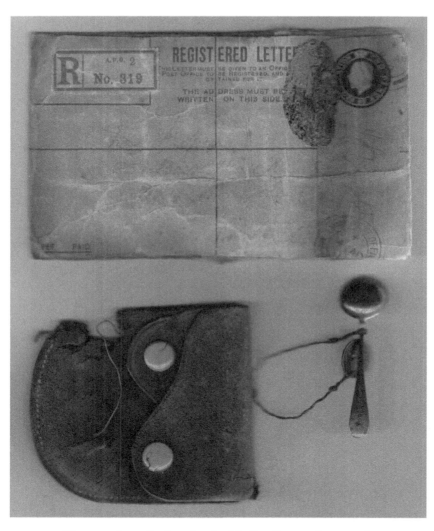

The envelope that arrived with Fred's powder pouch
and spoon (1916)

Fred Horsfall's naval certificate (1916)

Chapter 14: Arthur's War – 1915

Arthur Henry Spiers was seventeen years old, he worked on the docks with his father as a locomotive fireman. The pay was minimal, sixpence a day, and the work was incredibly physical, but since the start of the war every man, woman and teenager had been expected to either fight or work for the war effort. The recruitment age had been set at eighteen, and although the government had started a recruitment campaign across the country using the face of Lord Kitchener as their poster boy and had raised the maximum age from forty-one to forty-eight years old, they were still desperately short of fighting men.

Arthur was clever, good with numbers, and his reading and writing were excellent. Grandpa Frederick Horsfall had drummed the importance of those skills into each of his children and grandchildren. He had ambitions to be a journalist or maybe work in a bank, but obviously as the eldest of five children, he was expected to bring an income into the struggling household, so he left school at fourteen to work. He read the newspapers every day and felt strongly about the injustices he saw in his workplace. With extreme poverty in most of the East End of London compared with the obscene wealth of the few local land and business owners. His ambition was to document the living and working conditions of the various tradesmen and labourers in and around the docks that he witnessed daily. He felt Henry Mayhew's book written sixty years before, *London Labour and the London Poor,* now needed updating to reflect modern trades and work practices. Arthur was interested in politics and became an active socialist. He lived in the parliamentary borough of West Ham South, which became the first ever Labour-controlled borough in 1898 and returned an MP to Westminster in 1906. Immediately after the election, it was decided by the members of parliament elected to adopt the name 'The Labour Party'. The seats they won were based on their campaign for reform on issues like old age pensions and school meals. When the Old Age Pensions Act was passed in 1908, giving all men over seventy years old five shillings a week, Arthur could see changes being affected by the common man and was hooked on socialist politics for life. He could not wait until he was twenty-one and eligible to vote himself.

Arthur perceived injustice everywhere he looked in 1915. He still lived in overcrowded accommodation at Barge House Road, sharing a bedroom with two brothers and two sisters in their two-bedroomed house adjoining the river; the twins Doll and Harry were still only five years old. The toilet was in the yard and was shared with the family next door, and the water needed to be collected from the pump on the road outside. He had read in the papers since January about the Zeppelin raids on England, and then on the 31st of May, he witnessed them for himself over London. Huge airships dropping incendiary devices indiscriminating between military and civilian targets. Navigation was hit and miss, so they tended to follow the Thames and threw out ninety bombs each from the trapdoors underneath. Because of the random nature of the bombing, many women and children were also killed, and as a result the English press dubbed them 'baby killers'. These raids were so successful for a time that Germany saw them as the way to win the war. Germany decided to increase production of Zeppelins but had to cease sausage making as a result. The airtight linings for the hydrogen were made from the intestines of cows, as it took two hundred and fifty thousand cows to make one lining, there was not enough cattle to manufacture both. Eventually Britain developed an incendiary bullet to bring them down. Rather than break Londoner's spirits, these raids enraged men like Arthur, who viewed them as a cowardly attack on innocent women and children. Arthur was ready to enlist; government recruitment posters stating, 'It is far better to face the bullets than be killed at home by a bomb, join the army at once and help stop an air raid,' had convinced him. He would do what he could to protect his family. When he was old enough to be accepted, he would join up. Then, on 13 October, while he was drinking tea and reading the day's newspaper during lunch at the docks, he read the ultimate injustice and it enraged him beyond reason. Edith Cavell, a British nurse working in a hospital in German-occupied Belgium, treating both German and Allied casualties, had been executed by a German firing squad the previous day. She had been accused of treason for helping British and French troops escape to neutral Holland. The following day, Arthur went to the King's Rifle Regiment recruitment office in Woolwich and enlisted.

Arthur told the officer he was nineteen years old instead of seventeen, but to be fair, no one was really interested, and no checks were conducted as they were in desperate need of new recruits. He was accepted on 29 October and sent to Colchester to the 20th Battalion for training. At the age of seventeen, he was five foot seven and a half inches and physically fit. However, the sight in his right eye was only measured at six out of twelve, and his left eye was not much better, not ideal for a rifleman. He was declared unfit within three months and sent home. The Zeppelin attacks were still continuing in London, and by the time Arthur returned in January, he found number twenty-two had been hit by a bomb; death was getting closer. The house was the one Queenie had been living in before she moved away.

Arthur's sister Ivy had stayed in touch with Queenie, and they had sent notes and letters to each other recently. She had moved back to Barking last year, when her father had again been promoted, now to inspector, and she had called in to see Lucy Tillett while Ivy was there herself. Queenie asked after Arthur and seemed genuinely interested in what he was doing. Ivy thought this was strange as all the conversations she had witnessed between the two of them had always been less than affectionate. When Arthur came home from Colchester, she told him about Queenie returning to the area and asking about him. To her amazement, he was also interested in news of her; she was not sure she would ever fathom out teenagers. She told him Queenie was now living at the police station in Barking. Arthur did write a letter to Queenie telling of the damage to her old house and expressing his gladness that she and her mother were not living there at the time; he made no mention of her father.

Unperturbed by his rejection from the King's Rifles, Arthur again travelled to Woolwich and applied to join the Army Veterinary Corps. He would still be serving his country in France, but the fact he could not shoot straight was immaterial, and as he jovially told his mother, "I'll still be getting 1s 2d a day's pay, double what I got at the docks."

After his initial training at Woolwich Barracks, Arthur had his photograph taken in full uniform. He gave it to his mother so she could remember him while he was away and be proud of her son. It was at this point that the reality of going to war hit him, and his nerves showed in his photograph. The following week he was sent to the AVC base camp in Rouen in France; it was behind the Western Front and was used as a supply and recuperation station for the horses and men of the corps. The Battle of the Somme had started on the 1st of July, and within three weeks of his arrival in France, Arthur was sent to support troops on the front line. The Army Veterinary Corps were used to transport anything and everything that could possibly be pulled by a horse. Old gun carriages were used as wagons to take supplies to the soldiers on the front line and then bring casualties from the battlefields to the field hospitals and, from there, transfer those who were fit enough to travel on the horse-drawn buses for the next leg of their journey to the next medical facility. Alternatively, they were used to bring dead soldiers away from the trenches.

For the next two years, Arthur endured the hell that was the Western Front, moving from trench to trench, always with the same task. Whatever he transported with his horses and carts to the front, he brought the dead and dying away. He left the crumpled, mutilated bodies to be repaired and returned home or sent back to the front or alternatively buried where they were. He spent the rest of his time caring for his horses. The Spiers family in London served as Arthur's only distraction during these dark months. He wrote separately to each of them, both letters and postcards; the local French villagers did a roaring trade in sewing silk postcards in English. 'Happy Birthday', 'Happy Christmas', or a general goodwill message like 'Good Luck'. Arthur sent a postcard to each of his siblings for their birthdays and at

Christmas. During this period, he had more time alone than he ever had in his life. For the first time he missed the screaming kids, shouting and running about the house. A lot of his time was spent sitting around while he was at a hospital or cemetery waiting to be unloaded or for more supplies to be brought for him to load and take back for the troops at the front. He found he had a talent for drawing, and he found it was particularly satisfying to draw humorous characters and cartoons; he sent them home to the family and even sent one to Queenie. The last thing he wanted was for them to know the stress and anxiety he suffered day after day, week after week. Never knowing while he was at the front if the shell buzzing overhead had his name on it.

During August of 1917, while Arthur was performing a regular trip, delivering a supply of food to the canteen at the front, the enemy sent a bombardment of gas across the trenches. He donned his gas mask, which did alleviate some of the effects, but within minutes he was suffering breathing problems; his lungs were on fire, his eyes were burning. "Get your kit off right now, soldier, keep on your underwear." The sergeant was screaming to all the men around, "Get in the horse trough now, wash yourselves off, NOW!! Didn't I say keep those masks on?" Arthur did exactly as he was told, and on reflection, although he suffered some blistering of the skin and some breathing difficulties for the rest of his life, he escaped relatively unscathed. He was hospitalized for six weeks, mainly to stop the skin infection and to wash out his lungs. Many men who did not have a quick-thinking sergeant on hand died as a result, either from lung damage or, more commonly, the gas being absorbed into the woollen material of their uniforms caused extensive burns, which became infected.

On his discharge from hospital, Arthur was sent back to his unit. He was given light duties for forty-eight hours, then returned to the same front-line trench he had been injured in, not even two months previously. He went to the rear control room to find the sergeant to thank him for his help. A different platoon was on duty, and a second lieutenant emerged from the hut. "Can I help you, boy?"

"Sir, I'm looking for the sergeant who was here before, Scottish or Irish, I think, tall, ginger-haired," said Arthur.

The officer looked uncomfortable; he shuffled from one foot to the other and kept his eyes downcast. He was not a lot older than Arthur, but he was at least six inches taller. "Private, we have been on duty here a month now. The previous tenants vacated these salubrious premises and we could not miss the chance of upgrading our accommodation." His accent was not American, but Arthur had heard a similar voice before; Arthur guessed Canadian?

"Sir, I don't understand. Where have they been transferred to?"

"Sonny, all but two of the fifty good men of twenty battalion, King's Rifles were wiped out. It seems like Jerry had a last push, tried to break through our lines here. The boys held out till we arrived to shove Kaiser back where he came from. Sorry if they were your chums."

The death of one sergeant that Arthur had only met once for a few moments felt like a hammer blow to the solar plexus. He had seen more dead bodies in two years than any man not yet twenty years old had a right to, but the ginger sergeant, he was special, he had saved Arthur's life.

Arthur aged 17 (1915)

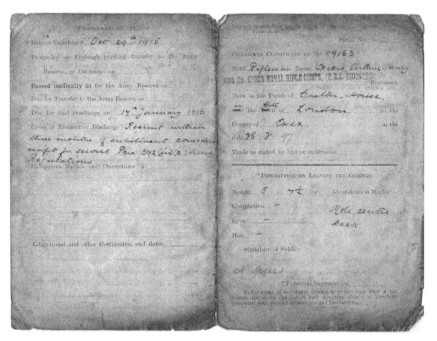

Arthur's King's Rifle Regiment certificate (1915)

Arthur's RAVC certificate (1916)

Two of the twenty silk postcards Arthur
sent home to his family (1916–1919)

Drawings Arthur sent home (1916–1919)

Drawings Arthur sent home (1916–1919)

Chapter 15: Arthur and Queenie – 1919

Ivy was helping Florence lay the table as Fred Percival would be home for tea soon. He had been working at the cable factory in Silvertown for four years now. It was heavy work, but he loved the camaraderie of the shop floor. Like his brother, he believed strongly in the rights of the workers, and the men there stuck together; if one of them had a problem with the management, they all had a problem with the management. It was April and just twilight, the red and green lights on the barges working the Thames on the other side of the wall were clearly visible, Dolly and Harry were still out playing hopscotch in the street. "Get them kids in will you, pet? I got a bowl of water 'ere they can wash their hands before tea," Florence asked her. Ivy wiped her hands on her apron. She was never happier than when she was in the kitchen with her mother, whether baking, cooking, or just peeling potatoes; Ivy loved being around food.

As she stepped into the front room towards the front door that was open, Harry came running indoors shouting, "Ma, Ma, there's a man here asked if yer were 'ome. He ain't the rent man nor the burial money man."

"Well, didn't yer ask 'is name, twerp?" said Ivy, irritated at her brother's stupidity. The man was standing still, arms by his side, staring at their house. "What yer wantin', mister?" Ivy called across to him. "Doll, yer get yerself in 'ere smartish, get them 'ands scrubbed."

The man was still standing silently, and Ivy thought he might be shaking a bit. She was getting scared, so she shut the door quickly. "Who were that, pet? Harry, didn't I tell yer to wash them hands? And do it proper today," chastised their mother.

"Dunno, Ma, some odd bod just standing outside looking at our 'ouse." "He's still there, Mum." Doll was standing on the chair, looking through the net curtains.

"I told yer to wash yer 'ands, now do it 'fore I give yer a four-penny one. I'll go sort 'im out." Florence was not a slim woman, big busted, wide-hipped, and big wayward hair piled on top of her head to keep it away from the food. When she opened the front door, she filled the void. "What yer doin' there, yer scarin' me kids?" Florence was never a real fishwife, but she was fierce enough when she had a mind to be.

The man had not moved. She noticed he was quietly sobbing; he had tears running down his cheeks, and his lips and shoulders were trembling. "Sorry, Ma, I never meant to scare 'em."

Florence let out an involuntary scream, the gaunt face and skeletal body she did not recognise. But the voice, the voice was unmistakable. She put her hand to her mouth as she dropped her towel on the red-painted doorstep and rushed to embrace him. "Oh, my boy, my lovely boy, what have they done to you?" Arthur dropped the small kit bag that was hanging from his arm, but he did not attempt to hold her; it would have been futile anyway, she had him in the tightest bear hug. She was never letting him out of her sight again. His mother was now sobbing as well as she led him towards the house. "Harry, Harry, go to the pub and tell yer pa our Arthur 'as come 'ome."

Harry did as he was told. As soon as he told his dad the news, his father abandoned his half-drunk pint and the two of them ran down the street. The sound of hob-nailed boots echoed along the road. They both charged through the open front door, where they were met by a stranger on a kitchen chair. His mother was kneeling beside him, and he still had her huge paw around his shoulder. Ivy, Doll, and Fred, who had arrived home in the middle of the commotion, all stood staring at the man they had not seen for three years. He had his elbows on his knees, seemingly afraid to look at any of them. Arthur did not kneel but hugged his son to his waist every bit as hard as Florence had done; it left the imprint of his wide leather belt buckle on his son's cheek. It felt so good that neither of them moved for an age, both sobbing, afraid if they moved, it might not be real.

Arthur had joined the army a young, upright boy, full of pride, passion, and fervour, with a spring in his step. He was apprehensive about what to expect but determined to make a difference to the war effort, determined to make his family proud of him. He had returned a physically gaunt and emaciated man; his face was sallow, and his eyes were lifeless; his back was stooped, his shoulders rounded, and he had flat feet that turned out when he walked. The effects of the gas had left him breathless. Mentally, Arthur was traumatised, shell-shocked, unable to cope with the normal day-to-day noises that he encountered on his return to London. Three years of the constant barrage of exploding shells, the unrelenting stream of dead and dying human beings that he saw daily, the gore and blood he woke up to and went to sleep with, the sights and sounds were constantly in his head, he could not rid his mind of them.

Fred spoke first, "S'pose you want yer bed back, bruv?"

It broke the ice, and all the children started talking at once, asking questions: "Where you been?" "What you done?" "Are yer gonna live with us again?"

"Enough now, all of you, sit down and have yer tea. You can talk to Art later." Their father had spoken, and calm reigned again, temporarily.

"Is it alright if I stay for a bit, Ma? Don't worry, Fred, I'm not used to a proper sleep nowadays. I can kip in the chair down 'ere."

Florence was mortified. She tipped her chair over, and it scraped across the tiled floor as she stood, rested her knuckles on the table and stared at Arthur. She looked a formidable sight. "STAY 'ERE?" she shouted. "Yer bloody well live 'ere, it's yer 'ouse. Don't yer even be thinking of living nowhere else, or you'll have me to reckon with. Do we understand one another, son?"

Tears welled up in Arthur's eyes again. He was still looking down at his plate, avoiding eye contact, but he now had his cheeky grin back again. "First time I ever heard yer use that language, Ma. Have yer been going down the pub with Pa too much while I been gone?"

Arthur's gentle recuperation continued for another four months. Sleeping in the armchair, walking the fifty yards to the riverbank, leaning on the wall, and watching the daily business of the river go back and forth. Occasionally mud larking on the foreshore, collecting odd remnants of a thousand years of river trade, maybe a clay pipe, if he was lucky, even an old coin. He would then return home to be fed home-cooked food and hear the stories everyone else had to tell of their day's excitements and tribulations. This was as exciting as he wished his life to be ever again. Gradually, over the weeks, he would tell a little of where he had been these past years but never what he had seen and done. All the stories he did relate were humorous or self-deprecating, telling tales of singing at night or drawing pictures to send home. Giving the impression to his younger siblings that he had been on a holiday, life had been a breeze. Obviously, his parents knew a quite different side. Arthur did not tell his parents the horrors he had witnessed, but they both talked to soldiers who had lived through the same war and had the same experiences, so they understood a little of what he had endured. The effects on his lungs of the gassing caused him long-term physical breathing difficulties. However, week by week, mentally he became more able to cope with everyday life, enjoying the sights and sounds of normal life again rather than dreading it would be the last thing he would ever see or hear.

One evening at dinner, Doll was telling the family how her first day had been at the new term at Elizabeth Street School. She was now ten and one of the older children; her sister Ivy was now thirteen and had just one more year left. "Betcha can't guess who is in my new class this year?" asked Doll.

"Harry?" answered Fred, who could not have been less interested in his sister wittering on.

"Course he is. We are twins, ain't we," she replied, unaware of the sarcasm. "But who else?"

"If yous don't tell us soon, Pa will be 'ome from the pub," said Fred.

"Yer, not yous, no such word as yous. How many times I gotta tell yer, Frederick?" interrupted Florence, now irritated with the whole confrontation. "Just tell us, pet, put us out of our misery."

Doll continued as if everyone were still interested, "There's this other girl, she's called Doll too, 'er real name is Doris Jennings, but they call 'er Doll, like me. That's the same name as that family what lived at twenty-two before the war, the one what Arthur fancied, that stroppy one. They just moved back round 'ere."

"Oh, Doll, yer do amaze me sometimes," said Ivy. "Doll Jennings has been here two years since. Reason you an 'er are now in the same form is on account of yer and our Harry being kept back a year cos yer ain't that smart."

"Ivy, that is enough," reprimanded Florence.

"Well, I don't care what yer says, me an Doll Jennings is friends," Doll said to end the conversation.

Arthur was now interested in the table chat. "Last time I heard, Old Man Jennings was out Brentford way some place," he prompted.

"Nah, made up to inspector on account of that funny handshake club he goes to, I reckon, an' he's come back to Barking nick, gonna rob money off some other poor sods."

That really was too much for Florence. "Frederick Percival Spiers, if you continue with language like that, yer father'll take 'is belt to yer. I'm not 'aving it, do yer 'ear me? Not in this 'ouse. It might be the done thing in yer factory, but yer ain't there now." Fred apologised, although his father seemed to him to be drinking himself to death, he doubted he would have the strength to strap him.

The following day, Arthur gave a note to Doll to give to Doris Jennings to pass on to Queenie. It asked after her health, her mother's health, and the health of her sisters; it stressed his gladness at her moving to Barking, which was only three miles away; it informed her he was home and enquired if she would care to meet him sometime. He heard nothing back for a full week, which he took as a rejection, he assumed she had met someone else while he was away. When he did finally receive a reply, it transpired Doll had only given her new friend the note two days beforehand, and she had forgotten to pass it on until Queenie had asked her sister if there was any news of Arthur Spiers coming home from the war yet. She eventually replied that she would be delighted to meet him again. How about Sunday?

Arthur and Queenie met regularly over the next couple of months, walking in the park or along the river by Barking creek, where Arthur would point out where the *Princess Alice* had sunk all those years before. Occasionally they would catch a bus to the Hackney Empire to see a music hall act, or as they liked to call it these days, a 'variety show'. Arthur's favourite was always Marie Lloyd. She was a bit risqué without being too rude, funny with plenty of double meanings. He knew every word of 'Don't Dilly Dally', all about a family doing a moonlight flit to avoid the rent man in the morning. Arthur had seen that happen enough times in their neighbourhood. Another favourite was 'Daisy, Daisy' or 'A Little of What You Fancy Does You Good'. Although they had read that her act in the West End was really rude, East Enders were really quite prudish and would not put up with a show like that. He drew Queenie pictures of some of the characters Marie Lloyd played after they had seen her perform. The drawing of a Geisha was the one Queenie liked the best after they had seen Marie Lloyd sing her song 'Geisha Girl' in full costume.

Arthur had gone back to his old job in the docks as a train fireman but had been given light duties because the soot got in his lungs, and he was not strong enough yet to shovel the coal quick enough. His father was still in the boiler-making workshop, so he got his son a job in there most days. He knew that he would not return as a fireman permanently, partly because he was not fit enough and partly because he now knew that was not what he wanted to spend his life doing. He had not endured the hell of France to return to the docks. The decision on his future was made on the first of December. His father, Arthur William Spiers, had a heart attack while at work and died immediately. He was only fifty-one years old but had travelled the world from Leicestershire to London via Birmingham and Australia. He had seen and done things around the world most normal East Enders only dreamt of.

Arthur accompanied his mother to Farrer & Sons in North Woolwich, their local undertakers, to arrange details of the funeral. Florence had been paying into a burial club for years, a penny a week for each of the children, tuppence for her and thruppence a week for her husband, in order to fund this day. To be buried a pauper by the parish carried such stigma that many really poor families that Florence knew went without food rather than default on their burial insurance. An irony that was not lost on her: had they spent that money on better food and warmer clothing, more of their children may have survived. Florence and Arthur chose an elm coffin with brass handles and a velvet lining, and an open coach and a pair of horses to convey Arthur to East Ham cemetery to be buried in the same plot as his two young children.

Queenie accompanied Arthur to his father's funeral, after which they started spending most of their spare time together, sometimes going to a pub or the pictures, since the weather was becoming less comfortable to go walking. Queenie did come to tea with Florence and Arthur and his siblings, but although Arthur always walked Queenie home, he refused to spend time at the police station while Inspector Jennings was there. He did visit for tea if Ernest was out, but that was normally only on a Wednesday when Ernest went to his weekly Freemason's meetings. Arthur tried his best to avoid Queenie's father as he had little or no respect for him. He had lived in the community in Limehouse when Ernest was a sergeant, and it was common knowledge if you went to Sergeant Jennings with a problem, he may sort it, but it would cost you.

This routine continued for the next two years. Arthur and Queenie were still inseparable, Doris Jennings and her younger sister Esther had become good friends with Arthur's sisters, and Ivy and Doll used to invite the Jennings girls to their house after school or at weekends. Like Arthur, his sisters were not comfortable at the Jennings home when Ernest was there. As young teenage girls, the four of them had no secrets; they gossiped to each other about everything that was happening in their lives, what they had done, the arguments they had with their families and with other children at school, the people they liked. The two families were becoming unavoidably intertwined; Florence could see that, Annie could see that, and Ernest could see it. Which made the events that happened one Saturday afternoon in September 1922 less remarkable than they should seem.

Arthur was at the police station in Barking to collect Queenie; they were heading to Green Street market. Ernest was not on duty;

he was checking some old newspaper reports about the Jennings family and a long-lost inheritance. The story was that one of Ernest's ancestors lent a friend some money, who went to America, made his fortune, and returned to England to repay his debt. By which time his friend had died, and to this day, the money was still in probate, waiting to be claimed by a descendant. It had been a month since Arthur proposed to Queenie, and she had accepted. Arthur nodded his acknowledgement of Ernest's presence and waited in the hallway. She was always late, and Arthur was always patient. Her father folded his papers and called out to Arthur in his slow drawl, "Well, come in here will you, boy?"

Arthur thought about refusing, then decided he would keep the peace and talk to him. He stood at ease, arms behind his back. "Inspector Jennings, how can I help you?" Arthur assumed it had something to do with the engagement.

"Ernest, please call me Ernest unless you see me on duty, of course, then it's Inspector." He chuckled at his humour.

"Yes, Inspector."

"How are you getting on at the docks? Anne tells me you are still having issues with your health." Ernest was now in interrogation mode, leaning in towards Arthur. "Well, see, I got a proposal for you," he continued. "Well, I decided it would be the best thing for our Queenie and you if you joined the Metropolitan Police. I can arrange for you to bypass the interviews and go straight in. On account of my rank and the service you gave our King and country."

Arthur ground his teeth in anger. "Would that be the rank of Inspector or Master of the Lodge?"

Now it was Ernest's turn to bristle, "Inspector of police, of course, any charity organisation I belong to has no bearing on my professional career whatsoever." He emphasised the last word, to leave this young upstart in no doubt who was in charge here.

Queenie breezed into the room just in time, unaware of the conversation the two men had just had, both men still staring at each other. "Hello 'andsome, you ready? Won't get me a new handbag bought standing around 'ere. Bye, Dad, come on, Art." Arthur nodded vaguely in her father's direction and left.

They walked hand-in-hand towards Barking Park, Arthur still seething at the impertinence of the man, to assume he could organise his life for him and, like everything else Ernest did, not strictly legitimately. Queenie mumbled the odd platitude, fully aware by now these two men would never be friends; civil was the best she could ever hope for. She had chosen the man she wanted to spend her life with and would have to work with the situation in hand. By the time they reached the long boating lake, Arthur had calmed down a little. "The dirty old bastard is right though; I do need a better job 'fore we marry. The money is rubbish, an' it'll kill me 'fore I make old bones. I'm no prospect for you as I am, girl."

"Don't you dare say that, Arthur Henry. I will not hear you talk yerself down. I would marry you if you 'ad no work, an' that's a fact, right?"

"You are right, you are always right. I know you would, nevertheless. I been thinking, I met my mate Frank, you know, from the army. I see him a while back an' he drives a bus outta Plaistow garage, an' he said I should work there. The pay's better, an' it ain't hard like the docks."

"Oh, Art, I do love you. You write better than any man I know, draw beautiful, and you're the kindest fella on this planet, but—"

Arthur interrupted her, "But what, what's so funny?"

"Well, Arthur, seems you ain't realised, you ain't got no driving licence. Driving a bus, you kinda need a driving licence; it's what it says on the job description." Queenie was now doubled up laughing at the irony of it. After a few moments, Arthur saw the funny side and laughed with her. When she had calmed down, Arthur explained slowly that they also had conductors on buses, and they did not need to drive. They needed to be smart enough to take the fare and give out change and be honest enough to hand it all in when they got back to the depot. He reckoned he could do all of those things pretty well. In January 1923, Arthur Henry Spiers left his job at the Albert Docks and joined the London General Omnibus Company as Frank Hammond's bus conductor.

It was the following February; Arthur had been a conductor on Frank's bus now for a year. When they returned to the bus depot after their shift, the inspector was waiting for them.

"Hammond, Spiers, my office, now." This was the third time they had been called into his office in that year.

"Sir?" they asked in unison.

"Yet again, I find that you have been going off route. How many more times must I warn you both?"

"Us, sir? I think there must be a mistake. Why do you think we may have strayed off route?"

"Hammond, do you think I am some sort of imbecile?" said the inspector, now getting seriously annoyed with the pair of them. "Spiers, does your mother still live down Barge house in North Woolwich?"

"She does, sir," Arthur replied.

"That's how I know it was you clowns. Spiers, you have been taking your mother back to her front door again after she's done her shopping."

Frank Hammond and Arthur both looked to the floor. It was Arthur who spoke first, "Who told you, sir?"

The bus inspector was now livid with both of them. "Who told me? Who the chuffing hell told me? No one chuffing told me, you pair of idiots. Barge House Road has a two-foot camber, it also used to have gas streetlights. I say used to because you two clowns ran down there yesterday with my bus, and because the camber of the road rocked my bus back and forth, it took out all the chuffing streetlights in the whole chuffing street." Arthur thought the inspector was going to explode he was so red in the face. They both looked to the floor again before Frank Hammond started to chuckle, which set off Arthur laughing. "Get out of my sight before I throw the book at the pair of you clowns; it'll come outta your pay."

As they shut the door behind them, they looked at each other and doubled up, laughing uncontrollably. One of Arthur's favourite jokes was to stand on the back deck of the bus and shout, "Aldgate, Aldgate." Someone would always say, "Are we at Aldgate East?" Arthur would say, "No, all get off, we don't go no further." He loved working on the buses.

Saturday, 14th of June 1924 was the day that Anne (Queenie) Jennings had dreamt of all her life, her wedding day. She wore a white silk dress and veil with a wreath of orange blossoms and carried a huge bouquet of pink carnations. Queenie had three bridesmaids, her sisters Doris and Esther, and Arthur's youngest sister Doll. Florence had made all of their outfits, they were silk dresses, with hats made of lace with pink ribbons, and they also had bouquets of pink carnations. Arthur's brother Frederick agreed to be his best man. The weather was balmy, not too hot, which was perfect for the girls' dresses and thick tights they were wearing. Ernest had agreed to host his eldest daughter's wedding at the police station house where they lived at Barking. They got married in the Wesleyan Chapel in East Street in Barking, and then the London General Omnibus Company provided a bus for the guests to travel from there back to the reception. Arthur's and Queenie's mothers had prepared finger sandwiches with egg, some cheese and some with boiled ham. There were also jellied eels, cockles, and oysters from the Thames, with jelly and trifle to finish. Florence and Ivy had made a two-tier wedding cake, using a recipe for the fruit cake from her mother's battered old book, and Ivy painstakingly smoothed the icing; it came out pretty well for a first attempt. The happy couple then took a coach to spend five days on honeymoon in Clacton-on-Sea before returning to the flat they had rented in Cecil Road in Barking to start their married life.

Marie Lloyd as her character 'The Geisha Girl' (1921)

Arthur Spiers's funeral invoice (1919)

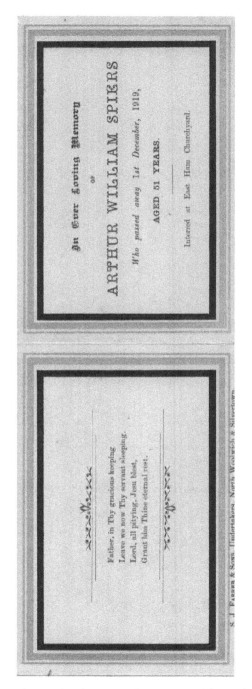

In Ever Loving Memory

OF

ARTHUR WILLIAM SPIERS

Who passed away 1st December, 1919,

AGED 51 YEARS.

Interred at East Ham Churchyard.

Father, in Thy gracious keeping
Leave we now Thy servant sleeping,
Lord, all pitying, Jesu blest,
Grant him Thine eternal rest.

S. J. Farrer & Sons, Undertakers, North Woolwich & Silvertown.

Arthur Spiers's remembrance card (1919)

Metropolitan Public Carriage Act, 1869
(32 & 33 Vict., ch. 115)
Road Traffic Act, 1930
(21 & 22 Gen. 5, ch. 43).

CONDUCTOR of Metropolitan Short-Stage Carriages

LICENCE No. 10051

I, being the authority having power to grant licences under the Metropolitan Public Carriage Act, 1869, hereby

licence *arthur Henry Spiers*

residing at *85 Rosex Road   Barking   Essex.*

to act as Conductor of Metropolitan Short-Stage Carriages.

This licence is issued subject to the provisions of the Metropolitan Public Carriage Act, 1869, and of any Order made thereunder by the Secretary of State relating to metropolitan short-stage carriages, and to the provisions of the Road Traffic Act, 1930, and of any Order or Regulation made thereunder by the Minister of Transport so far as those provisions are applicable to conductors of metropolitan short-stage carriages.

This licence shall remain in force for one year from the date hereof unless sooner revoked or suspended.

Trenchard

Commissioner of Police of the Metropolis.

Dated *1st* day of *March* 193 *3*

THIS LICENCE, if not sooner revoked, suspended or renewed, must be surrendered to the Commissioner of Police at the Public Carriage Office, 109, Lambeth Road, London, S.E.1. on the *first* day of *March* 193 *4*

Date.	Memorandum of Change of Address.	Entered at Office of Commissioner of Police.

Photograph of Licensee.

A H Spiers

Signature of Licensee.

Arthur's conductor's Licence (1933)

Arthur as a conductor (1924)

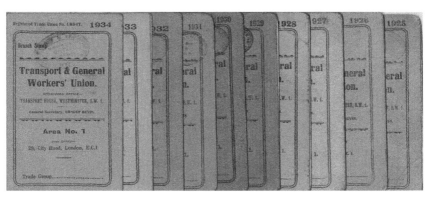

Arthur's TGWU cards (1925–1934)

WEDDING.—The marriage of Mr. Arthur Spiers, eldest son of Mr. Spiers, of North Woolwich, and Miss Annie Jennings, eldest daughter of Police-Insp. Jennings, of Barking, took place recently at the Wesleyan Church, Barking, Rev. Philip Phillips officiating. The bride, who was given away by her father, wore a dress of white silk with veil and wreath of orange blossoms. She carried a bouquet of pink carnations. The bridesmaids were Misses Doris and Esther Jennings, sisters of the bride, and Miss Doris Spiers, sister of the bridegroom, who were attired in white silk dresses and carried bouquets of pink carnations. Mr. Fred. Spiers was best man. The hymn, "The Voice that breathed o'er Eden," was sung. After the ceremony a reception was held at the home of the bride, and was attended by a large number of guests.

Arthur and Queenie's wedding picture and newspaper report (1924)

Chapter 16: Back to Bentley – 1925

Annie Jennings and her sister Jessie sat in the foyer of Barking Police Station, a modern building that was purpose-built fourteen years ago, a solid Edwardian design, airy with large windows. It was a busy station with three inspectors, two sergeants and twenty-six constables. The sisters were surrounded by bags and a travelling chest. The removal van had left yesterday, with the rest of their belongings, in truth, not much to show for twenty-five years of marriage, however much of that time had been spent in furnished police accommodation. The cases left were mainly overnight clothes and personal effects the family would need immediately when they arrived in Great Bentley. Ernest was saying his goodbyes to his comrades and was checking everything was in order. The car was ready to take himself, his wife, her sister, and his daughters on their journey to Essex. Ernest had spent the last weeks reminiscing over his career, its highs and lows. He was particularly proud of his promotions – to sergeant in Limehouse, to station sergeant in Brentford, West London and onto his inspectorate at Barking. He had made a great many contacts during the years he was a member of the Freemasons and was proud of the local influence he wielded. However, now was the time to move back to his home village.

The war had just started when he returned to East London as an inspector. He did visit some of his old haunts in Limehouse; however, by now, they had become less popular, and by the end of the war, with the returning troops looking for work, the Chinese and Asian labourers were extremely unpopular. This in turn led to anti-Chinese riots in the area, smashing shop windows and damaging laundry equipment. Within six months, the opium dens had all but smoked themselves out of existence, and the Limehouse region was more poverty-stricken than when he first arrived in 1906. He remembered the good times he had spent there before war broke out, the relative peace he had created in the bubbling cauldron of the Limehouse Basin and the profits he had made that made him smile.

Jessie had moved in with her sister after the death of their father. Her deafness made it awkward for her to live on her own, and Annie was extremely pleased to have her company, not to mention her help in bringing up her three daughters. Jessie had now spent four years living with Annie and Ernest, at times happily and at other times not so. However, the one constant in her life had always been her sister, and she would do absolutely anything she asked, and what Annie wanted was for her sister to chaperon her daughters and any friends that they brought into the house. At the beginning, Jessie thought she had misunderstood her sister's sign language, but it soon became clear Annie felt unable on her own to protect vulnerable young ladies who came into Ernest's household.

William Jennings had passed away in 1920, and his will had stipulated his youngest son, Ernest, should have first preference to buy his house. Ernest had always said it was his wish to return to Poplar House in Great Bentley on his retirement. He took up this option and paid his surviving brother, Arthur, and his sister Grace, one hundred pounds each for the property. However, he had left it empty for four years. Queenie had married, the expense had been far more than he had budgeted for, but it had been a success, so he considered it worth every penny. Since he was now an inspector, his pension would be three-quarters of his annual salary; it amounted to two hundred and fifty-two pounds a year. He had completed twenty-six years' service, and it seemed the perfect time to return to his childhood home. The clapperboard cottage with the rickety roof and the now not-so-white picket fence. The huge garden with the gooseberry bushes, all the fruit trees and the beehives. It all needed a bit of tender loving care and a lick of paint, but he would have all the time in the world to redecorate it.

One last time, Inspector Jennings received the salute from his men, turned and took his seat in the Wolseley next to the driver. He was forty-eight years old and was about to embark on the next stage in his already illustrious life. He would continue the rat and mole-catching tradition of his father and grandfather and rebuild the beehives so he could teach his wife Annie how to make the famous Jennings's honey.

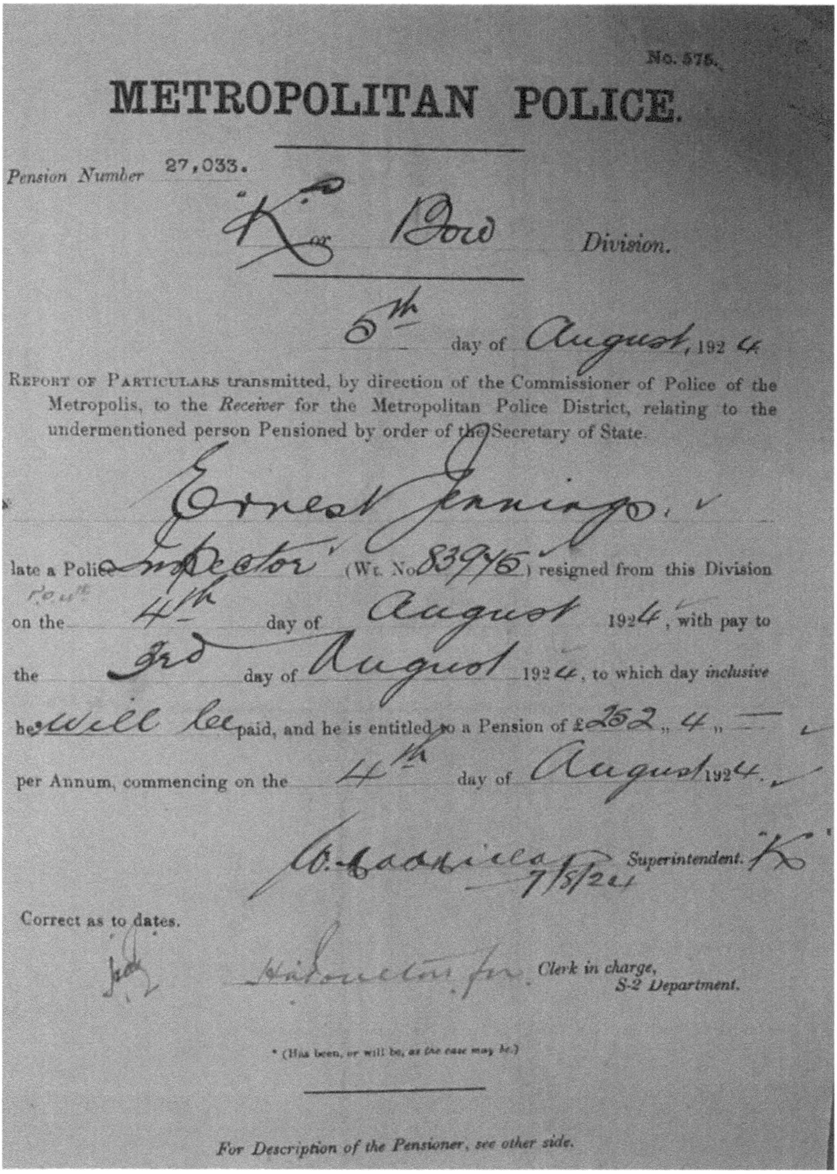

No. 575.

METROPOLITAN POLICE.

Pension Number 27,033.

"K" or Bow Division.

5th day of August, 1924

Report of Particulars transmitted, by direction of the Commissioner of Police of the Metropolis, to the *Receiver* for the Metropolitan Police District, relating to the undermentioned person Pensioned by order of the Secretary of State.

Ernest Jennings.

late a Police Inspector (Wt. No. 83946) resigned from this Division

on the 4th day of August 1924, with pay to

the 3rd day of August 1924, to which day *inclusive*

he will be paid, and he is entitled to a Pension of £252 „ 4 „ –

per Annum, commencing on the 4th day of August 1924.

Superintendent. "K"

7/8/24

Correct as to dates.

Clerk in charge,
S-2 Department.

* (Has been, or will be, as the case may be.)

For Description of the Pensioner, see other side.

Ernest Jennings's retirement papers (1924)

Description of the Pensioner, &c.

	Pensioner	Wife
Date of joining the M.P. Force	9th May 1898	
Length of Service in the Force	26 Years completed	
Age on resignation	48 Years complete	
Remuneration at date of retirement { Pay	£ s. d. 4. 6 0	
Been Aid		
Special Duty Allowance		
Detective Allowance		
If Single, Married or a Widower	Married	
Description of the Pensioner and wife — Height	5 Feet 9 Inches	5 Feet 5 inches
Hair	Brown	Brown, turning grey
Eyes	Grey	Blue
Complexion	Fresh	Pale
Where and when Born	Great Bentley Essex	Farningham Kent
	On the 29 October 1849	On the 6th January
Where and when Married	at Eynsford Kent On the 7th January 1894	
	(As shown on the Marriage Certificate.)	
Particular Mark, Defect or Infirmity	Nil	Nil
Pensioner's Signature in full	Ernest Walter Jennings	Witness J. Summerton
Signature of wife (if any) in full	Annie Jennings	Rank Inspector Police Station Barking

* These signatures must be witnessed by a Police Officer of the rank not below that of Inspector, or by the Police Officer in charge of the Police Station where the pensioner last served.

Chapter 17: Richard Howell Comes and Goes – 1924

Florence Annie Spiers had become a widow at the age of forty-four. She lost Arthur, the man who was once the love of her life before the drinking took hold. By the time he died, he was not the man she fell in love with on that park bench. Five years later, she still had four children living at home. However, her son Arthur would be married and gone in a few weeks, she would miss him terribly. The twins, the youngest of her children, were still only fourteen years old, Ivy was working away from home, and Fred, when he was not working, was at the church. Florrie had matured into a vibrant, energetic, kind lady, known all along the street as the one to turn to if you needed a favour. Maybe if you needed a child looked after or to borrow a pot or someone to accompany you to the undertakers and fill in the forms required to bury a parent or woe betide a child, she was the neighbour to turn to. She was always ready with a smile and a cup of tea if she thought you were in need; although she was one of the poorest in the road, she would share whatever she had.

Since her husband had died, she threw all her considerable efforts into the welfare of her children. To be honest, before he died, she was besotted with their care. She now worked three jobs: mending clothes for customers, buying clothes to mend and sell, mainly from the markets, and a cleaning job in the Woolwich Arsenal firearms factory over the other side of the river. For this last job, she had to start at six in the morning and work for four hours every day except Sundays. Florence would take the first ferry of the day from North Woolwich across the river and walk the mile to the factory on the other side if the buses were not running. During the summer months, this was a beautiful, peaceful, tranquil time of the day before the hectic hustle and bustle of daily life started in earnest, with the sun rising along the Thames, silhouetting the Greenwich Observatory, high on the hill in the distance to the east. However, it was a different story in the winter. The bitter, freezing wind ensured no sane person enjoyed the walk along the river foreshore. On the rare occasions the wind was occupied elsewhere, the rain or sleet, ice or snow stepped up to the mark and caused the local population misery and pain.

The Woolwich Ferry had been established in 1889 as a free service, although there had been a toll ferry running across this part of the river since the fourteenth century. The paddle steamers that were still in use were thirty-five years old and prone to regular breakdowns. As a consequence, each ferry was appointed a chief engineer and a mate on board along with the captain and at least two more crew to ensure the boats did not get stranded mid-stream and block the life blood of London. The first ferry of the day was sparsely used most mornings, a few vans coming back from the markets or tradesmen about their business early, but not much other traffic. In winter, the crossing was bitter; every part of the ferry was cold, the handrails were still frozen as were the decks, there was no shelter for foot passengers from the wind blowing from the east along the river. Florence, who had always had an issue keeping her hair in place, found this time of year a particular challenge.

"You look right cold, my luverly."

Florence looked over toward the wheelhouse to see a portly sailor in a captain's uniform, about her age with a kind smile, grinning at her. It turned out the uniform was a chief engineer, not a captain. She was huddled against the rail with the collar of her woollen coat pulled up as far as it would go, her hair had been plastered across her face by the damp wind, and her eyes were watering with the chill. "Yer right, I seen a queue of brass monkeys at the welders on my way 'ere this morning," she replied, keeping her head braced against the wind.

Chief Engineer Howell howled with laughter, his belly wobbling uncontrollably and his shoulders bobbing up and down. "Got a pot o' chocolate on the brew, I 'as, if you wanna warm them hands, my luverly."

"Well, I don't usually go below with decks with sailors I ain't been introduced to, but seeing as you got pips an' I seen yer these past weeks, and on account of I'm freezing out 'ere, I reckon it'll be OK," Florence replied as she followed the engineer carefully down the metal stairs to a cramped but warm room. It had an ancient black iron coal stove with a pot balanced precariously on the top. A small desk with a few papers, and a closed door, where it sounded as though the workings of the ferry were situated. He handed Florence a battered tin mug and proceeded to fill it from the pot off the cooker. The steaming chocolate smelt divine; she was hesitant to taste it in case it was disappointing, so she just cupped the mug in her mittens, unsure of what to do next.

"Sorry, my name's George. I'm the engineer on this 'ere ferry," he introduced himself.

"Florence. You'll forgive me if I don't shake 'ands as they're too bloomin' cold, but thank you all the same," she answered with a coy smile, turning her head slightly but not taking her eyes off him. That was it; George was hooked, and she reeled him in like one of the eels the rivermen pulled in by the dozen every day. Florence was never quite sure what she did, she was no spring chicken, but men found her enchanting. She sipped the hot, sweet beverage; she was not disappointed.

George Howell, he later confided, was born in Falmouth in Cornwall and had been christened Richard George, but he preferred to be called George. He had been an apprentice boatbuilder in the town's vast dockyard, then gone to sea as a ship's engineer after he had been indentured. After an unsuccessful marriage, largely spent at sea away from his family, it has to be said, he decided it was time to settle down as a bachelor somewhere new. He had gravitated to London, a place he had visited many times during his long naval career. Since their first meeting, the morning chats over hot chocolate were the highlight of his day; he even bought Florence a new mug with no chips. For Florence's part, she started brushing and tying back her hair neatly for these early morning dates, well as neat as she ever managed it. George realised a few weeks later what an effort this took and what an honour she was bestowing on him. In early May, George popped the question. Neither of them was getting any younger, and if they planned to spend any time together, they had better get a move on. George had met her children, and they seemed to like him well enough, so they set a date for the second of July, two weeks after Arthur's wedding, at the Woolwich Registry office, local to George, who was living in one room in Charlton, just down the road, at the time.

Ivy was eighteen when her mother met George; she was working in a large house in Vanbrugh Terrace, on Blackheath Common, as a live-in nanny to the child of Captain Ronald James Moses Holliday and his wife, Alice. He was a retired army officer, and her family had a title and some money somewhere in the not-too-distant past. They had one son called Christopher, who Ivy grew to adore, and the feelings were reciprocated by him and his parents. She became a surrogate daughter to the family, joining them on their frequent holidays and attending their family occasions. Ivy continued to look after young Christopher and the family until the boy left to join the forces himself.

Frederick Percival Spiers was the second son of Florence Annie and Arthur William Spiers, two years younger than his brother Arthur Henry. He turned eighteen years old as the war finished in 1918 and was not therefore required to enlist. He was a hardworking, honest, loyal young man, better working with his hands than his head. He joined a small cable manufacturer in North Woolwich, near his home, when he left school. It was taken over in 1925 by the Standard Telephone Cable Co., and he worked as a cable packer with them for the rest of his life. While there, Frederick met a young cable winder called Marilyn; they had a lot in common. Both grew up with a parent who preferred drinking to spending time with their families; Fred's was a father who spent more time in the Bargehouse pub than he did in number thirty-three. Marilyn had a mother who drank too much gin; she did not bother with pubs, she kept her own company, drinking indoors alone. Most days of her life, Marilyn would come home from school or, later, work to find her mother passed out in the chair. She was the eldest and had become an accomplished cook by the age of twelve out of necessity, making sure her father and siblings were fed. They both talked of their dislike of alcoholics and the harm the family suffered as a result, not least the economic cost of drinking to a family's budget. She had been brought up to accept swearing as a normal part of the East End language, whereas Florence had ensured no matter how poor her family was, certain values would be adhered to in any circumstances. One was no swearing; one was no drinking alcohol in the house, and the most important rule was that what she said was law. Fred and Marilyn spent their lunchtimes at work together; they talked and talked about the things they had in common, so it seemed only natural to get married. In the meantime, Fred had put a good word in for his sister when the factory was looking for more staff, and she worked there for a year. Doll was put in the same department as Marilyn, and they worked alongside each other. Because of the link with Fred, they were briefly friends. Doll could not stand the foul language, and although at first Marilyn apologised, eventually she told Doll to shut up and live with it. Doll left her job the following week.

The plans for the wedding were progressing, although Fred and his family had little input. Fred was told what to wear, where to be, and at what time; this suited him fine. He asked Arthur to be his best man, which he reluctantly agreed. He had tried on numerous occasions to persuade his brother to look for a more suitable bride, but to no avail; Fred's mind was made up. The big day arrived, East Ham church was not full, but the front three pews had a scattering of both families and a few work colleagues from the factory. Fred wore the suit he had bought for Arthur's wedding two years earlier, but his mother and both sisters bought new dresses and hats. Florence was on the front pew with George, and she reflected on how her life had changed so quickly. Arthur was married and now had a son, nearly a year old, who was the apple of her eye. His smile was contagious, he only had two front teeth. He reminded her of the milkman who came round her street on his horse and cart. The old man barely had a few wisps of hair left, one tooth on the top and one on the bottom. No one could understand a word he said through the whistles and spit, the same as Ronald. She smiled to herself, just thinking of baby Ronald did that for her. Ivy was still living in Blackheath, and she had never seen the girl more contented. When she came home, she did not stop talking, telling them she had done this or that. She glanced behind, and Ivy and Doll had their heads together, catching up on some serious gossip. Florence heard them mention Doll Jennings, and she thought she heard the word pregnant; she would remember to ask the girls about it later. Doll Jennings was only seventeen and had no boyfriend that she knew of. They looked embarrassed when they realised their mother was watching them. Ivy had been given two days off for the wedding, and Florence wondered how that captain's family would manage without her as she seemed to run the whole household. It would seem strange after Fred left, just the twins still at home although they were now seventeen. Harry had started working for the railways and was rarely there. She wished he would let her know when he was coming home for tea, but he flitted in and out like it was a hotel; she assumed he was working, but it was probably best not to ask what he was up to. Harry always had a lot of friends, he always had a lot of girlfriends, sometimes a couple on the go at the same time, she supposed that was the advantage of railway work; you were never where a girl could track you down, she smiled again.

Now Dorothy was a different one again, although a twin to Harry, they could not have been more different; she had extraordinarily little confidence and few friends. Florence expected she would live at home for ever. Dorothy was the one she worried about. What would she do with her life? Would she ever meet a man? She was not sure she had ever spoken to one, other than her brothers. Well, Mr Jennings, of course, but Dorothy always said he made her flesh creep. She was not used to men touching her, and he seemed to touch her more than was necessary. If Doll or Esther Jennings were not there, she had refused to go in. Dorothy missed the Jennings sisters, but she was glad the inspector had moved a long, long way away.

Frederick and Arthur were standing in front of Florence, sharing a joke. Arthur punched his brother playfully, she did not catch what was said, but they both laughed. Fred checked his watch for the forty-seventh time; Marilyn was now twenty minutes late. The congregation turned as the big oak door behind them creaked open, but instead of the bride, it was her father, on his own. He strode down the aisle toward Fred. "She ain't comin', stupid cow 'as changed 'er mind." He turned towards the wedding guests, "an' you lot might as well…" He realised at the last minute where he was and stopped himself telling them where to go with a string of expletives. "No point in you lot sitting about, nuffink left to see 'ere." He turned and left as quickly as he arrived. The rest of Marilyn's family followed him out of the church at a run; not one made eye contact with Fred.

As they reached halfway down the aisle, her mother was heard to say, "She'll pay for this day, every bloody penny. I never been so embarrassed."

There was a moment of stunned silence before the chaos. Doll began crying first, Florence ran to hug her son, and the vicar, who was as shocked as the rest of them, shook Arthur's hand and apologised. It was no fault of his, of course, but it was what he was trained to do. Ivy was hugging her sister, trying to console her. Their friends and co-workers left slowly, some going to Fred and touching his arm with a nod or a word. What could anyone say to him? Fred sat on the pew, stunned. He kept repeating, "Why? Why? Why?"

After the obvious recriminations and anger, the Spiers family left the church en masse and returned to their home in Bargehouse Road. Florence broke one of her golden rules and opened the bottle of sherry she had been keeping for next year's Christmas pudding. She poured them each a small shot, although it barely covered the bottom of the glass, as they only had tall water glasses in the house. Fred sent a note to Marilyn the following day but got no reply. He went in to work as usual on the following Monday, hoping to see her, hoping she would explain her decision to him; however, Marilyn sent a note of resignation into work and never returned to the Standard Telephone Cable Co. Fred never heard from her again.

Florence and George got along admirably. They spent time together, they made each other laugh, they went on day trips and holidays together, getting coaches around Britain and even travelling onto the continent to Belgium and France. Now Fred was living at home, along with Dolly and Harry, and George was bringing in a regular wage from the ferry and not spending it at the pub before he got it home and Florence still had two of her jobs, the family was as financially well off as they had ever been. Life was comfortable, but as was always the way for Florence, that was all about to change.

Florence woke up at five o'clock as usual, sat on the edge of the worn mattress and glanced over her shoulder, but George was up already. She pulled on the pink dressing gown that he had bought her last Christmas and tied the belt around her now ample waist, she then padded downstairs to put the kettle on the stove to make him a cup of tea. She found him sitting in the armchair by the grey embers of last night's coal fire. She passed by without waking him, lit the stove in the scullery under the kettle that he had filled with water before they went to bed last night in readiness for the morning brew. George very rarely slept in the chair, maybe if he had a cold or was unwell, unlike her first husband, Arthur, who slept in the chair most nights, too drunk to make it upstairs. George was in his pyjamas with his dressing gown on and a pair of threadbare socks. She thought he must be freezing with no fire left to keep him warm, so she decided to check if he needed a blanket over him. Florence called his name and then gently touched his shoulder.

She jumped back in shock, at once transformed back to that eleven-year-old girl who had discovered the other George, her baby brother, dead in the top drawer all those years ago. He looked so peaceful, eyes closed, his head gently resting on his chest, with his legs crossed at his ankles. George was sixty-six years old, not a bad age for most men who had lived the hard life he had; however, she was not ready to live without him yet. They had only known each other four years, and she felt a warm, comfortable contentment with him she had never experienced before. Florence sat on a wooden chair opposite him, with her elbows on her knees, looking at his slack face. She could hear the kettle restlessly whistling in the background, demanding her attention, but she was not ready to deal with it just yet.

Richard Howell as a chief engineer (1924)

In Ever Loving Memory

of

RICHARD GEORGE HOWELL

Who passed away 4th February, 1928,

AGED 66 YEARS.

Interred at West Ham Cemetery. Grave No. 74569 M.G.

Peace! perfect peace! with loved ones far away
In Jesus' keeping we are safe and they;
It is enough, earth's struggles soon shall cease,
And Jesus calls us to Heav'n's perfect peace.

S. J. Farrer & Sons, Undertakers, North Woolwich & Silvertown.

Richard Howell's remembrance card (1928)

London County Council.

Elizabeth St SCHOOL _____ DEPT.,

Woolwich L.C.C. ELECTORAL AREA,

20 . 7 . 1920 .

MEMORANDUM from the HEAD TEACHER.

To

Testimonial [SUBJECT.]

Ivy Spiers has been a scholar in this school for three years. She is generally well-behaved and polite in manner. She is especially good at figures.

Florence Lemare .

Ivy's Elizabeth Street School testimonial (1920)

Chapter 18: Wolsey Avenue – 1929

Frederick had been working at STC for fifteen years since he was a fourteen-year-old boy; the episode with Marilyn caused him to shy away from women's company as much as he could, he was sure he would be a bachelor forever. His mother was still in despair after the loss of her second husband; she was also convinced she would never meet anyone else who would make her as happy as George had in those short years she had known him. Doll had never shown any intention to leave home either. Now was the time, Fred decided, now was exactly the right time for them to move away from the docks. The Corporation of London had just built a new housing estate in East Ham, three miles away from the incessant noise and smell of the river, three miles from Bargehouse Road and the memories of two dead husbands. Three miles was not far enough away, though, to rid Fred of the nightmares of 'that' day.

The agent showed Frederick and Florence around number 72 Wolsey Avenue. It was in the middle of a terrace of identical houses, with a front garden, a low wall and a gate painted green, the same colour as the front door. As they walked across the threshold, they saw stairs on the right of the hallway; there was a door to the left and another in front along the narrow hall. There was a round Bakelite switch on the wall for the electric light, each room had one. The door on the left led to a square room with a tiled surround fireplace; it had a window looking out over the front garden. The first thing Florence noticed was the wooden picture rail around the walls; she would be able to display the paintings her brother Frederick had brought her back from Malta. They continued down the dark hallway to another square room with a matching tiled fireplace. It had a larder cupboard in the corner and a glass back door with windows either side looking out onto a garden at the back. Both Fred and his mother headed to see the view. They had never had a proper garden before. Florence once lived in a house with a yard, where you could hang out washing in private, but never a garden. The pair of them were grinning at each other like lunatics from Bedlam. The agent saw this reaction every time he showed a family from the docks one of the houses on this new development.

They turned and went through the doorway to the right into the kitchen. It was actually a real kitchen, not a scullery, it had a deep white sink with running water from a tap on the wall, and it also had a gas stove. The agent had the trump card up his sleeve. He moved across to the long tin worktop, and with a flourish, he lifted it up to reveal a bath with taps and running water as well. Florence brought her hands to her face; Fred thought his mother was going to cry. She tugged a loose strand of hair behind her ear that had fallen across her face. An indoor bath, whatever next. They walked out the back door into the garden. As they turned around to the right, attached to the house was a door, and when they opened it, they saw a flushing toilet. "We could build a lean-to across here, Ma, out of glass, so it is covered from the back door to the lavvy; you wouldn't get cold in the winter." Florence smiled as she walked to the fence at the end of the garden; she was shaking, it may just have been the chill wind blowing across the marshes. She stepped onto a box and looked over, there was an empty field behind. Part of the reclaimed marshes, the agent said, "Never be any good for building on." The three of them went back inside and investigated the upstairs. There were three bedrooms, two large rooms and one small one, each with a small black fireplace but no other furniture.

They thanked the agent for his help, promised to call into his office tomorrow, and left. On the way home, they sat on the bus in silence, both imagining them living there. Florence turned to Fred and said, "I have so many questions, son. Yer need to be true to us both 'ere. Firstly, have we really got the money for this? Next, have yer thought that yer factory is a five-minute walk from our house now, or 'alf hour on one o' these buses twice a day, back and forth." Frederick Percival Spiers was anything but an impetuous man. He had meticulously worked out his sums, worked out his wages, and he had spoken to a man he knew from the church on Sundays, who arranged mortgages. He had ridden this same bus four times to try it and knew he could leave his new house, walk to the bus stop and still be in work in thirty-eight minutes. Florence laughed; she should have known her son better.

Fred agreed a price of three hundred and sixty pounds for their new home and signed up to a loan with the United Juvenile Order of Total Abstinent Sons of the Phoenix; he would repay it back over twenty years. Florence, Fred, and Dolly moved in during the first week of December 1929, and Harry arrived a week later, grumbling that, "You lot can try and run away from me, but I'll find yer." Florence laughed and hugged her youngest boy, then Doll proudly showed him around his new home. They drew up a rota for the new bath; Fred had it Mondays, Florence Tuesdays, Doll Wednesdays and if Harry was home, he had it Thursdays. On those evenings, the rest of the family were expected to make themselves scarce for a couple of hours to give the bather some privacy.

That Christmas was monumental for a number of reasons. It was the first time any of the Spiers family had celebrated the festivities in a house they owned; secondly, Christmas 1929 was the first time the family met Henry White. Harry, as he was known, was a soldier in the Scottish Rifles for nine years. Since leaving the regiment, he was working in the Woolwich Arsenal, the huge armaments factory that Florence used to clean. Henry Robert White joined the army in 1918 and after his training was sent to India and Iraq, then back to India, before he was discharged and started a second career in the gunpowder yard at Woolwich. He was a short man, barely five foot six, but muscular with a cocky, rolling gait. His hair was still cut 'army' short, as he had got into the habit, and with his big blue eyes, looked much younger than he was. Harry always had a story or a joke; most were just a little bit naughty, barracks humour as you would expect from an ex-soldier. They always made Dolly blush, and Harry and the rest of the family then teased her mercilessly. Ivy had met Harry while she was shopping in Woolwich market with young Christopher. Harry and his brother George had left work at midday on Saturday and were on their way to the pub. They cut through the market when they turned a corner and knocked Christopher over, straight onto his bottom in his new trousers. They stopped to pick the boy up, make sure he was not hurt and apologise. Ivy later recalled that George did most of the talking and apologising to Christopher while Harry stood there with a stupid grin and could not take his eyes off her. She was twenty-three years old, with a self-assurance and confidence born from running a household and caring for a young boy at such a tender age herself. She was attractive, with an impish face and a quick smile. Her hair was short and neat, and she prided herself on looking smart enough and dressing well enough not to embarrass the Hollidays when she was seen out with them.

The next few years were good for the family. Arthur and Queenie moved from Cecil Road in Barking to Essex Road, still in Barking and only about a hundred yards away. This house was similar to the house Fred had bought in Wolsey Avenue; it had electric lighting and running water in the kitchen, but it did still have an outside toilet in the garden. Arthur was still a conductor on Frank's bus, and they got a transfer to the route that went through East Ham, past Wolsey Avenue, so their bus took Fred to work. Most mornings, if the inspector was not on board, he dropped his brother off right outside the factory gates.

Fred had kept the promise that he made to his mother and built a glass and wooden extension on the back of the house so the new flushing lavatory was accessible without going outside into the garden. Fred developed a love of gardening; he dug over the rubble plot that was the back garden and laid a square path around a bed in the middle. He then planted roses and lavenders in that and edged it with bricks that had been left stacked up against the back fence and shaped fruit and vegetable beds down each side with the bricks as well. He had read books on garden design and seen gardens that had been laid out by Capability Brown in the eighteenth century, and he was particularly impressed by photographs of Versailles; his mind liked the symmetry of them.

Gardening and football became Fred's two great loves; he spent his Saturday afternoons in the winter watching West Ham

United at the Boleyn Ground. Since they had moved to their new ground in 1904 from Blackwall, he had occasionally watched them, first going with Arthur when they were teenagers before the war, but now he had moved house, he was only two miles away, and he could walk there easily every week. The team were relegated to division two in 1932 and stayed there for the next twenty years, but Fred's support never wavered. Week in, week out, rain or shine, he cheered them on. By 1933 the garden was looking spectacular; he found he had green fingers, and whatever he planted grew. He read books and taught himself how to take cuttings and plant seeds. He used his new glasshouse extension to grow-on his trays of new flowers and vegetables before they were ready to plant outside. Fred bought a paraffin fire to keep the young shoots safe from the frost, which Florence and Doll thought was fantastic; it kept them warm when they passed through to the toilet.

Ivy and Harry came over for tea one Sunday, which in itself was not unusual, but there seemed to be an atmosphere that Fred could not fathom; they were nervous, which was definitely not like Harry. They had been there an hour before Fred could bear it no more. "So, what is going on with you two, sitting there perched on yer chairs, like Joey in his cage." Joey was their green budgerigar who was intently watching them from his cage. Ivy and Harry exchanged furtive glances.

Ivy spoke first, "We know what you think of weddings, our Fred, and we do understand that, but yer know me and Harry was planning on getting wed, well, we was wondering if yer would agree to us having the reception here afterwards."

No one spoke for nearly a minute; the pause was driving Ivy crazy. Finally, Harry broke the silence, "If you're not happy, Fred, we understand, we will have to find somewhere else."

"When you two thinking of?" Fred finally said without looking directly at the couple, the pain of his aborted wedding obviously still raw after all these years. Florence noticed he had not rejected it out of hand. Ivy explained that they could not marry until May, which is when Christopher was going into the army. She had agreed not to leave her job until she was no longer needed. "Right, this is the deal. If our Ma is happy to cater it, I'm happy, only one condition." This was the moment Ivy was dreading; she looked at Harry again in trepidation. "The wedding will have to be on a weekday when I'm out at work."

Ivy was not sure what she had expected, but not that. She thought Fred might make an exception and attend her wedding. "You not gonna be there at all, our Fred? Me and Harry was hoping you would give me away."

For the first time, Fred looked directly at Ivy. "Sorry, sis, that ain't gonna happen, best you ask Art or Harry. You can have the do here, an' I hope it's a good un, but I won't be there myself, best you don't waste an invite."

Ivy ditched her Spiers name and became a White on Tuesday 30th of May 1933, when she wed Harry. Arthur was honoured to walk her down the aisle at St. Marys church in East Ham, although his father of the bride speech consisted of him saying how pretty she looked, how proud he was of her, and thank you all for coming, less than one minute. Florence broke golden rule number two for the second time when she allowed alcohol in the house, which Arthur insisted he needed to get through his speech. Florence did spend most of the wedding reception in the kitchen making tea in a yellow, tin commercial teapot she had borrowed from the church. Frederick kept to his word and did not come home until the last guest had gone. Although he spent the weeks building up to it avoiding all the planning talk by tending the garden, which everyone commented on how neat it looked. He did not attend another wedding for the rest of his life. Arthur took the next day off work as a day's holiday, which was just as well as he could not really remember much of the previous night; he was not a serious drinker, unlike his father.

Arthur and Queenie's second son, Anthony, was born on March 4th the following year, nine months and four days after Ivy and Harry tied the knot.

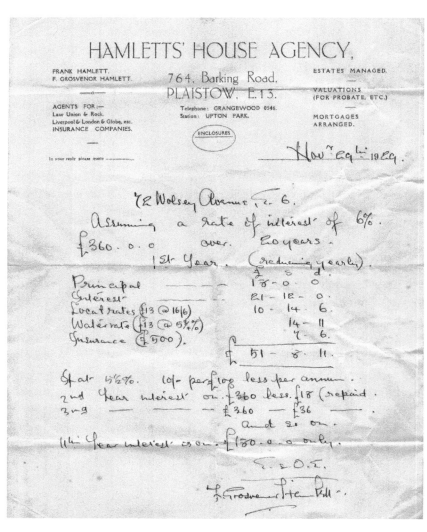

Wolsey Avenue estate agency invoice (1929)

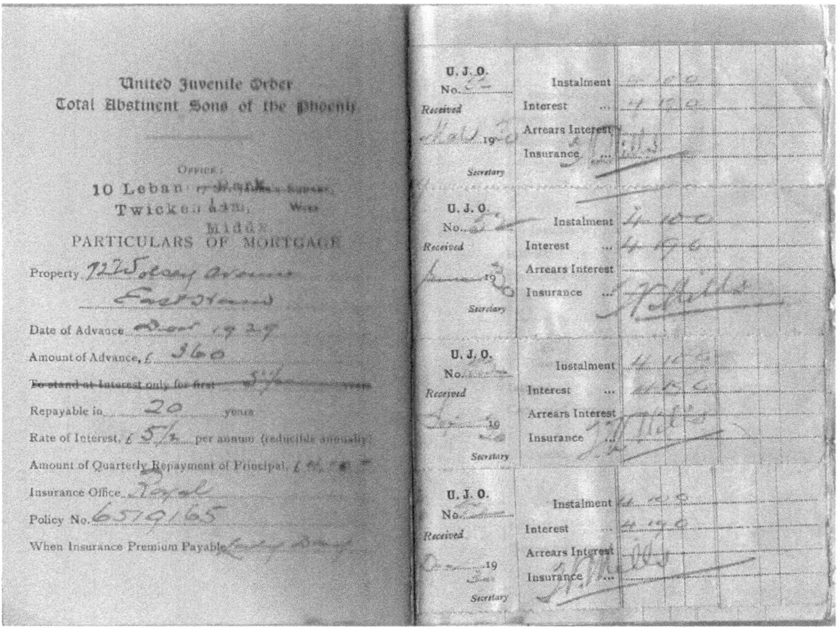

Wolsey Avenue mortgage book (1929)

TELEPHONE GRANGEWOOD 1430 (14 LINES)

COUNTY BOROUGH OF EAST HAM

Town Hall,
East Ham, E.6.

E. W. JOSLIN.
TOWN CLERK

14th June 193

Dear Sir,

<u>Temporary Building Licences</u>

    I am directed to inform you that the
Council at their last meeting decided to renew the
licence granted for the Temporary Building used
for growing plants and storing bicycles at the rear
of 72 Wolsey Avenue, East Ham, E.6
for a further period of two years, subject to you
filling in the enclosed form of application.

    Failing your entering into the enclosed
undertaking within 14 days from the date hereof,
the building must be removed forthwith.

        Yours faithfully,

        Town Clerk.

Mr. F. P. Spiers,
   72 Wolsey Avenue, E.6

Application to build a lean-to onto Wolsey Avenue (1931)

156

Ivy and Harry's wedding photograph in the garden of
Wolsey Avenue (1933)

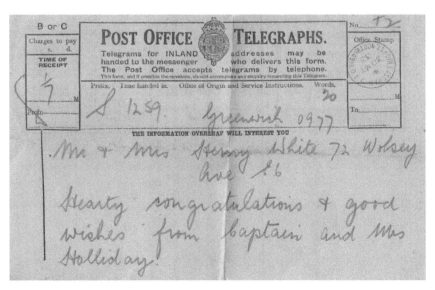

Congratulations telegram from Captain and Mrs Holliday (1933)

Chapter 19: Frederick's Letters – 1933

Florence exchanged letters with her father in St Louis every week, as she had since he arrived in the United States in 1909, him signing off each one with his customary 'Nuff Sed'. Now the family remaining in England had moved to Wolsey Avenue with its garden, Grandpa Fred had started sending them seeds and advice on growing everything from hibiscus to melons. Frederick had never planted a living thing until he moved into 1456 Hamilton Avenue in St. Louis, Missouri, in 1926. It was an apartment block which had a shared garden. Frederick Thomas Horsfall was now seventy-five years old. He was born in one room in a tenement block in Wapping and now lived in a one-room basement in a tenement block in St. Louis. However, the difference to Frederick was that now he had access to a garden, it had become his passion. He was still fit, he worked two days a week, and he painted his one room himself, grey on the upper walls and dark green on the lower. He said he 'painted the scullery the same, the kitchen the same, the dining room the same, the living room the same.' All his living accommodation painted the same colour.

He had time now to reflect on his life, particularly during the winter months when he had little to do in the garden. His greatest pride were his children; they had also caused him the greatest pain. The three children he had lost, firstly George, who was not even a year old. Secondly, Rose, who he had sent to America with her sister when she was only fifteen. She got married when she was just nineteen and had a daughter the next year and a son two years later. The family lived in St. Louis until 1911, where her husband Thomas was the vice president of a livery and undertakers. They then moved to a farm near Buffalo in Iowa, two hundred and seventy miles away. They had only lived there a year when Rose caught pneumonia and died after ten days' illness; she was twenty-nine years old. It was her wish to be buried at St Peter's cemetery in St. Louis. The funeral was arranged for the sixth of April, four days after her death, so her coffin was sent on the train accompanied by her husband and children. Unfortunately, April in that part of the world is usually a very wet month and 1912 was no exception. After heavy rain, the Cairo levee burst its banks, delaying all railroad traffic for twelve hours, causing Rose to miss her own funeral. The burial eventually took place the following day. Four years later, in 1916, he lost his third child, his eldest son and namesake Frederick Thomas, who died fighting for his country in the Battle of Jutland in the Great War. Frederick was always an optimist, and he thought of himself as a lucky man to have five surviving children, well, seven if you count his two daughters from his second marriage, still living in London, although he had little contact with them.

Frederick had decided in 1921 to become a naturalized citizen of the United States of America after the Emergency Quota Act was passed, which only allowed a certain number of immigrants from any one country to stay in the US. He wanted to ensure he could not be sent back; by then he was seventy years old and had no intention of returning to England. He was amused to have to confirm he was not an anarchist or polygamist; technically, he was still married to Charlotte Geeves, but he stated he was a widower. He was a little concerned to have to renounce any allegiance to King George V, although to be fair, the King's father Edward VII was still on the throne when Frederick had left England in 1909.

In late May 1933, Ivy decided to send her grandfather a slice of her wedding cake. In the letter she enclosed with it, she described her husband, Harry White, and told Frederick of her love for him, all his positive attributes and how happy she was. Frederick was delighted to receive the cake, and that one thoughtful act resulted in a series of letters between the two. In his reply to her, he gave her some marital advice. He wrote, 'I am going to tell you what your mother's mother's mother told me when I married your mother's mother, she told me to be sure and not forget. It takes two persons to make a quarrel, get it, well don't forget it, the pair of yerz.'

In December of 1933, Ivy knitted her grandpa a jumper, which she sent to him in a parcel. While he was delighted to receive the gift, that he called a slipover as it had no arms, he was livid with the American post office who charged him ten cents extra postage. As a response, his next letter to England he addressed to both Florence and Ivy to save himself five cents; he only had to buy one stamp instead of two. Now he had another focus for his letters to Ivy; he would ask her washing instructions for his new 'sweater'. Although he would only need to wash it occasionally as he was keeping it for best, to go to the stores, not for work, and he would take it off when he got home in case he needed to put coal on the range and 'smudged it'. Each letter to Ivy and Harry contained at least one tip for growing plants. Hibiscus was a favourite of his, and he sent them some white hibiscus seeds in a letter in April the following year, with instructions to soak them well in a cup of cold water before planting them. He called these tips his 'fairy tales'. He was concerned Harry was not planting enough vegetables and recommended multiplying onions as a good starter plant. His one horticultural failure was gooseberries; he complained that the ones grown in America are always sour, 'belly achers', so asked his daughter Florence to send him some English seeds to plant. Unfortunately, they would not take in the soil and weather conditions of St. Louis. He did blame her for scalding them before she sent them, though.

By July of 1934, the depression in America seemed never-ending; the banking collapse of the previous year now affected almost everyone. Frederick had contracted influenza and had now been made unemployed at the age of eighty-three into the bargain. He described his basement as the 'coolest place in St. Louis, bar the ice plants'; however, the thermometer had not dropped below eighty-five degrees. Grandpa Frederick wrote to Ivy and told her of people collapsing because of the heat in the streets; they were taken to hospital where some of the fitter ones survived, the weaker ones 'pegged out'. Frederick's eternal optimism allows him to conclude that had he not been laid up with the flu and been unable to work, he may have been outside and been one of the 'pegouts'. He concluded that letter with the usual 'Nuff Sed' but also added. 'I am T.I.R.E.D.' Ivy replied, concerned about his health, but did cheer him up with the news that Harry had followed his instructions to the letter, and the white hibiscus seeds he had sent them were growing nicely in the garden of her new home in Plumstead. This elicited a two-page letter by return with advice for cutting them back before the frost and packing around the base with grass cuttings to protect them. He repeated the same advice on the end of each letter thereafter.

Frederick was particularly excited when a neighbour, Mrs Hohman, who had kindly taken to looking after him while he was ill, swopped one of her bedsteads for an ice box for him. It cost him thirty cents a week in ice, but it kept his food fresh, so he saved that cost and more. Refrigerators had first been mass-produced in America seventeen years before but were still so expensive. Frederick had read about them making their own ice but did not know anyone who owned one. The new technology was irrelevant to him, partly the exorbitant cost but mainly as he had no electric sockets in his basement room, only a light.

The last letter Ivy received from her grandpa was in June 1936. He apologised for not replying sooner but had been busy in the garden after a particularly hard winter. He was upset that the climbing roses he had planted three years ago were almost killed by the frost but determined to spend the next three years getting them back into condition. He would cut them back to the roots and hope they would eventually make the ten feet tall they had been before the winter. He had again tried growing gooseberries and was now desperate for Harry to write to the gardening column in a London newspaper to get any advice he could on growing them successfully.

Ivy had also sent a slice of her wedding cake to her uncle Harry Horsfall and his wife, Christine, after her marriage. They had bought a house in Villa Ridge around forty-five miles from St. Louis in 1916 when he had a Buick dealership there. It had gone out of business in 1926, and Harry had started work in a local chicken hatchery. Although at the time of Ivy and Harry White's wedding, he had been transferred one hundred and seventy miles away to another branch of the company in Evansville,

Indiana. So, he was living away from home five months a year, working seven days a week from five in the morning until ten thirty at night, but in these depressed times, at least he had a job. When Christine came to visit him, she bought the wedding cake with her, and although it was broken, they ate it and wished her and her new husband lots of success. Three years later, in 1936, Harry had been transferred back to the local hatchery in Metropolis Hills, which was only a forty-mile daily commute from his home.

In July 1936, Frederick was again taken ill with another bout of influenza. Mrs Hohman had since moved away from his building to the other side of the city to be near her husband's work, so he had no one to care for him. Harry and Christine took him to their home in Villa Ridge to nurse him.

Frederick Thomas Horsfall died there on the thirtieth of July 1936 at the ripe old age of eighty-five.

He was buried two days later at St. Peter's Cemetery in St. Louis. Nuff Sed.

Flood, Delaying Train, Causes Postponement of St. Louis Funeral.

MRS. ROSE EDMONDS.

DELAY of a train coming to St. Louis from Buffalo, Ia., due to floods, necessitated the postponement of the funeral of Mrs. Rose Edmonds, which was to have been at 2 o'clock yesterday afternoon. Mrs. Edmonds died at Buffalo Tuesday from pneumonia, of which she had been sick for ten days. Her body was accompanied to St. Louis by her husband, Thomas R. Edmonds, and two children, who were to have arrived at Union Station at 7:30 o'clock yesterday morning, but arrived instead at 5 p. m.

The funeral will be at 2 o'clock this afternoon from the residence of Robert Skene, 3962 Evans avenue, to St. Peter's Cemetery.

Mrs. Edmonds was 29 years old and was born in London. She came to the United States with her parents fifteen years ago. Besides her husband, her father, Fred Horsfall, 1011 Allen avenue; a daughter, Evelyn, 13 years old; a son, Ronald, 11; a brother, Harry Horsfall of Cairo, Ill., and a sister, Mrs. P. J. Randall of Morenci, Ariz., survive.

Mrs. Edmonds' brother left Cairo Wednesday night on the last train before the break in the Cairo levee, which has stopped the railroad traffic.

Mrs. Edmonds was formerly a resident of St. Louis, her husband having been employed by the Scott Livery and Undertaking Company for thirteen years. A year ago the Edmonds family moved near Buffalo, Ia., to a farm.

Newspaper clipping describing Rose's funeral (1912)

The Letters

1. 14/6/33 Thank you for wedding cake, mother's mother's story, takes two to quarrel. Lived there seven years.
2. 09/10/33 Harry painted their bedroom; Frederick painted the whole flat. Culinary skills.
3. 02/12/33 Thank you for the jumper, 81 years old, still works 2 days a week. More culinary skills.
4. 04/12/33 To Florrie/Ivy/Harry, wash instructions for the jumper. Save five cents. No more fishing.
5. 13/12/33 the Lord's Prayer in a telescope, happy new year.
6. 21/1/34 Save new jumper for best. Corns.
7. 16/4/34 Corn farming, white Hibiscus, gooseberries.
8. 07/7/34 85 degrees in basement, people dying in the street, had flu, T.I.R.E.D
9. 19/8/34 Hibiscus, melon growing lesson, hollyhock seeds, 84 degrees in the shade.
10. 24/9/34 Dolly teetotal, Hibiscus lesson, fairy tales.
11. 25/11/34 Sore eyes, 84 years old, (actually 83), Hibiscus lesson.
12. 04/8/35 Mrs Hohman exchanges a bedstead for an ice box, 30c a week for ice. Some fridges make ice by electricity, 90–96 degrees in the shade. People had died, Hibiscus lesson.
13. 24/9/35 Sorry Ivy and Harry had not been well, more seeds, fairy tales.
14. 20/1/36 Saving postage.
15. 12/3/36 Weather, Mrs Hohman is moving.
16. 04/6/36 Hardest winter ever, apologies for not writing, busy gardening.

1456 Hamilton Ave St Louis Mo
June 14/33

Dear Mr & Mrs Whitix

recieved your Lovely Wedding Cake
with Compliments yesterday washure
glad hear from you and hear the glad
News and if there is any good in wishes
you have mine Bushels of them; But "Listen"
I am going to tell you What your mothers
mothers mother told me when I married your
mothers Mother; see where we are getting;
she told me to be sure and not forget; it
takes two Persons to make a quarrel; get
it; Well dont forget it; the Pair o joy; I guess
I shall soon be hearing from Mother, then I shale
get a few more Particulars; but dont Let
that interfere with your writing me I shall
allways be glad to hear from Both of

you; because if you are my grand
Daughter your husband must be my grand
Son. Well I hope you Both will enjoy good
health. I believe that this old Depression
has not come to stay; it has been coming for
a long time and it will take time for
its recovery; but if we have good health
we can scratch along and fight it so watch
your health. I expect to have better health or
better comfort anyway. the old Lady were I
am living has put new flooring in my
Kitchen and I have laid pipes under the Lawn
connected with the sewer to carry the water
off the roof into the sewer instead of my
Kitchen that has been soaking in for 26 years
I have been fighting for it for 7 years when I
first came here to live I ty wanted it; it is done now
Nuff sed for this time only Lots of Love to Both and
Best wishes from Grandpa Fred Horsfall

1456 Hamilton Ave St Louis M O u. S A.

Oct 9/33

Dear Ivy & Harry

recieved your welcome letter was sure
glad to hear from you and to know that
you were well: but you need not think
you are everybody because you have a
Painter in the Family; because you
have one right here in u. s. a. I have pain
my bed room also; Grey the upper walls dark
Green the lower. the sculleay the same.
the kitchen the same. the Dunning room
the same. the living room the same, it did
not take me long to do the Painting because
the whole business is one room and I made
such a good job of it I am going to apply for
the job to Paint the Ceiling of Forest Park

if I do not get the job I shall be warm
in my suit of rooms this winter I have
fixed up the old kitchen range I can Bak
anything in it, if I can get anything to
Bake, and I can even cook water
without burning it, But Lister: you say
Harry's been Painting your bedroom, now
that does not sound to me as if there is much
work about for him to find time to Paint
bedrooms. Well Ivy I think I will take
you up on your Roposition about the
slipover and many many thanks am enclosing dimentions of the Animal. I owe
Mom a letter I recive just before I recieved
yours I thought I would answer yours first
so you could get to work I recieved a letter
from Harry and Chriss last week that is the fire
I have heard from them since the 3rd of July Nuff
with Lots of Love and best wishes from
Grandad Fred Horsfall

14 56 Hamilton Ave St Louis
M O
Dear Ivy
it is rather late in the season
for Xmas or Birthdays at least
my Birthday and I dont deserve
another, I always was too soon
or too late but in this instance
I hope I am not too late to thank
you for that nice Birthday
Present you sent me, you see:
I have only 19 more years to go
to make up the 100, they say
the first 100 years is the hard

and after that it will be
easy so I am looking forward
for easy street, not that I have
anything hard to complain
about I only work two days
a week the rest of the time
I fill in burning other peoples
coal and carrying out the ashes
and cleaning the dust out
of my kitchen oh I nearly forgot
the cooking, I can cook why
I can Boil a Kettle of water
without burning it, Nuff Sed
again thanking you I will conclude
with Lots of Love and best wishes
from Grandad F Hassfall

1456 Hamilton Ave St Louis MO
Dec 4/33   U.S.A.

Dear Flossy & Ivy & Harry
recieved your Beautiful Sweater
this morning many many thanks and
it fits fine; just as if a Professional had
made it, but when you write again tell me
how to wash it without shrinking it
I do my own washing so I will be able
to take care of it I mailed you a
letter on Saturday but I dont think
they will collect foreign mails till
tonight so mabe you will get the two
together. Now the reason for me writing
the both of you in this letter is; because
the Darn; swindleing Money grab
put 10c extra on the Postage of your
Parcel because they could not

change any more for Duty so I am doing this to get 5¢ of my own back. Ivy will be calling on you so it will not cost you anything and I shall have the satisfaction of swindling the swindlers, am enclosing the Receipt for the Package so you can see how they mix things up Nuff Sed. Hope you are all well; you have had all the colds and the fevers you can get; so perhaps you will be satisfied for a while. I have been lucky not caught anything yet, but I do not go fishing any more will Close for this time with many many thanks and Lots of Love and best wishes to all from Dad Fred Horsfall

1456 Hamilton Ave St Louis Mo. u.s.a.
Dec 13/38

Dear Mys & Harry

Just a few lines to wish you Both
the whole whole wish of the year
and May all your troubles be little
ones; and Lest we forget; I am mailing
you a reminder in the shape of a telescope which I hope you recive ok; with the
Lords Prayer Printed on a Pinhead and
again I have to thank you for that
Nice warm slip under or over which
you like they call them Sweaters
here; and again I am wishing you
a Happy Xmas and a Bigger and Brighter
and Better New year is the earnest
wish of Grandpa Fred Horsfall

1456 Hamilton Av St Louis Mo

21/1/34

Dear Ivy & Harry

just a few lines in answer to your welcome letter was glad to hear you liked the little keepsake it is so small one can easyly lose it, I suggested to Dolly that if she put a ring thru her nose and tie a string to it she would not lose hers and could not possibly forget: thanks for Advice on slipover, I do not wear it only to go to the Stores, but when I get home ones is apt to find the furnace wants some coals on it, as the old Coal range in my Kitchen and then it is likely to get smudged, I have an old Blue one that I wear to work; that I had given me over 8 years ago, there are several places where the day light comes thru but it keeps me warm with a jacket over it. glad

to know you were well and Happy
but do you know the old saying it
if you move during the first twelve
months of Housekeeping you will
keep moving hereafter, I have not
heard any iron dispute that get unless
it is when one is asleep; was glad to hear
you had gotten closer to Harrys work
it is better to pop home and get a bit
of Home cooked food at midday
Was glad to know you had a good
time at home with Mom at Xmas.
I had a good time as far as eating and
drinking was Concerned; but all
alone but Santa was real good to
me again this year; and I am feeling
fine; all but; my sunday Corn; that is
a Beast; but I am very thankfull I
have not gotten two left feet; ruffshed
With lots of Love and best Wishes
for a Better New year from
Grandpa Fred Horsfall

1456 Hamilton Ave St Louis Mo u.s.a

April 16/34

Dear Ivy & Harry I

recieved your welcome letter was

true glad to hear from you and that

you were both alive and kicking

I am fairly well for a kidd; with the

exception of my corn it has been

making me hop some to-day I realy

believe I am going to get another corn

out of the same cavity; that will

make four; I think I had better start

farming corns but I do not think I

should get much of a market days

I am enclosing a few White Highbiscus

they grow from three to four feet high

and bloom a large white flower; they

are very hard seeds and require soaking

four or five days in a cup of cold water

I sent mom some and forgot to tell

to soak them will you remind her

but vegetables are before flowers
tell Harry to try and get some
multiplying onions they are winter
onions you put one little set in the
ground and you get five or six in
the ground and a bunch of sets for
your next sowing (on Top) besides your green
onions for winter use. last week I
sowed nearly four pounds of grass
seed and today (Sunday) it has rained
all day and looks like all night
the first steady rain since I sowed
the seed, last summer I got Mom to send
me some large red ripe Gooseberry s
but I think she must have scalded them
washing them none of them came up
better luck next time. they grow the
Gooseberrys here about the size of your
small finger nail and allways green
and sour. Nuff sed for this time. Only
Lots of Love and Kisses and best of
Wishes from Grandad & Horsfall

1456 Hamilton Ave St Louis Mo
U.S.A.
July 7/34

Dear Ivy & Harry
recieved your welcome letter
some time back and Beg to inform
you I am not talking any more
excuses for not writeing oftener
so am paying you back by makeing
you wait: but this time it is
compulsory. I have had a severe
attack of Flue and it has left
me like a half Dead man and the
Heat helps it along. I see in the
Papers mom sent me that London is
sweltering with the Heat at 77 deg
I am liveing in a half underground
Kitchen the coolest place in St Louis
(Bar Ice plants) and my thermoter has
not registered below 85 all the time
I have been home sick; it has been
up to 89 in the Shade. People have been

droppings in the Streets from the Heat
they take them to Hospitals some recover
some Peg out. I reccon I am one of the
Fortunate ones; if I had been well
I should have been out at work and
might have been one of the Pegouts
better Luck next Summer. I do not Know
what is the matter with Chrissie & Harry
I have not heard from them for over
two months. am encloseing a part of
Mom's Packet of Mask Melon seed for
Spring soming I dont remember seeing
any when I were home. you can get the
directions for Planting from Moms Packet
packet. Hightliscus needs plenty of
water. loosen the ground round them
before watering. Nuff Sed I am T.I.R.E.D
so will conclude for this time with
Lots of Love and best wishes
from Grandpa Fred Harspall

1456 Hamilton Ave St Louis M O

Aug 19/34 U.S.A.

Dear Ivy & Harry

recieved your welcome letter
was sure glad to hear from you
and to know you were both OK in
health and was glad to know your
Highbiscus were coming along they
may not bloom this year but they
will next and the stems will be
stouter and stronger but I would ad
vise when they die down this fall to
cut them back to three or four inches of
the ground then cover them with old
grass cuttings or leaves to protect
them from frost they will come up
strong next year but the Melons
need rich growing I would advise break
ing the spot were you are going to plant
your seed now; and dig a hole and put
in all your old rubish that will not

179

off the vegetable garden dont let
your Pea vine and Bean vine get
dry before you bury it that will
rot and feed the ground then before
you plant your seeds dig up all the
old rotten stuff and mix in more
you plant your seed and you will
(have some Melon)
of course horse or cow manure would
be better. Here endeth the first Lesson
on Melon growing. but save your seeds
if you get any. am enclosing a few
Hollyhocks seeds to help the flower
garden Nuff sed on gardens. I am still
mending but oh so slow we had a nice
rain that cooled it off some but my
thermometer has gone up from 78 after
the rain to 84 well I guess we will
to put up with that till we get the
other 10 degrees to make it 94. I do not
know any more Fairy Tales to tell so will
close with Lots of Love and best wishes
from Grandpa Fred Harspall

1456 Hamilton St Louis M O
Sep 24/34
Dear Ivy & Harry

recieved your welcome
letter was sure glad to hear
from you and know you were Both
OK; had a letter from Mom the same
mail as yours; she tells me she has
turned Nurse; and you have turned
Cook; and Dolly what has she turned
OH I know a teatotaler, Good for her
It is getting quite cool here I have
had a fire in my kitchen range but
that is excuseable for me I have
gotten a fresh Cold from somewhere
but the same old cough to keep me
awake at night; AH Well it is no
use getting old if it doesent make
any difference. Your Hightbiscus
need plenty of water when growing
when they change color that look

181

they have finished for this season
when the leaves die off cut the
stems back to two or three inches
then cover up with some dry leaves
or grass cuttings to protect them
from frost they will bloom next
year dont forget to put musk
melon in ther spring as soon as
the frost is over, it would pay
Harry if he could get some
and burie it were you think of manure
sowing melon seed then all you have
to do when you sow your seed
dig up the manure and mixe with
the soil if you put in manure right
away it will rot by the time
you plant seeds; I am encloseing
a few more but save your seeds
well I dont know any more
Fairy tales to tell you this
time. only: Lots of Love and
best Wishes from Grandad & Horsfall

1456 Hamilton Ave St Louis
MO U.S.A
Nov 25/34

Dear Ivy & Harry
recieved your welcome letter of long
ago; it is my turn for excuse's this
time; I owe everywon letters I
have had band my eyes, that is
what it feels like; anyway
they are much better or you
would not get this I have been
useing a weak solution of Boric
Acid that seems to do them more
good than anything I have tried.
you ask about the Pullover wether
it is worn out; it is a Dandy; and
I washed it last fall and put
it away for the Summer; do you
know I think I would a success as
a washerwoman I do my own wash.
and I done a good job on that Pullover
and kept its shape fine you say

183

I must not think about getting old, you forget I am an Englishman I cut out an add in one of your Papers of an Englishman 106 years old advertiseing for a job Active as at 40. I have heard the remark that an Englishman does not cut his wisdom teeth Till he has shed all his others. now that 106 year old man must have shed all his wisdom teeth to be advertiseing for a job at his age; why I have only 16 more years to go to make the 100 after that it will be easy. Keep your Hightiscus protected from the Frost and it will Bloom fine next summer I have cut mine down close then cut the Stems into pieces about two inches in lenth and put them over the Roots for Protection Dont expect good results if you do not feed anything Lots of Love and Best wishes to Both from Grandad Fred Hovshall

1456 Hamilton Ave St Louis Mo
U.S.A.

August 4th/35

Dear Ivy & Harry

recieved your welcome letter was
glad you liked Chimpanzee from
the Zoo; I let Mrs Hohman read your
letter she was ticled with it and had
a good Laugh over the kisses; a week
on two back she exchaged a Bedstead
for an Ice Box for me so my food
would not spoil this hot weather
I thought that was very kind of her
but it costs me 30 cents per week for Ice but
it saves some of that in food. a family
could not do without Ice here; some
families use 50 lbs of Ice per day, some
have refrigerators that makes its own
Ice by Electricity. it has been hot

here the thermometer registered for nearly two weeks from 90 to 96 in the shade; Lots of people have collapsed in the streets; some have died from the heat. I have written Mom and asked her to send a Birthday Card to Mrs Hohman something like you sent me. her Birthday is on the 25th of September I thought perhaps you and Dolly and Mom could put one each in the envelope for her kindness to your old Grandad She would appreciate that more than anything, she was tickled with that letter from Mom she had never recieved a letter from so far away. my Highbiscus has been in Bloom just a week now and is 6 feet High I hope you get some Bitter Sweet I cant not from seed and if your melon's dont turn out good I have some good seed for next year but if they do turn out good save your seed Nupp sed; only Cantelaups will not grow without manure. Lots of Love and best wishes from

Grandpap H Housdale

1456 Hamilton Ave St Louis MO
                        U, S, A.

                    Sep 24/35

Dear Ivy & Harry

recieved your welcome letter was
sure glad to hear from you and to
know that you were both able to
sit up and take a little nourisment
as usual; four or five meals per
day and a Bite of supper, glad to
hear your Highbiscus is blooming
mine are done blooming, when yours
are done blooming and the seed pods
turn brown snip them off save them for
next year or sow them this fall were
you want them to grow the old ones
will come up again next Summer

187

I am encloseing a few more melon
seeds in case yours do not come
to anything, I believe you can grow
them there if you feed them: they
should grow as large as your two
fists put to-gether; if you feed them
and water them they are worth the
trouble. I cannot understand why I
cannot
grow Bitter sweet I have planted them
in the fall and again in the spring
but nothing doing they make a nice
indoor Table decoration all the winter
and keep their bright red color with
out water, I do not know any more
Fairys tales to tell this time: only:
I am fairly well and hope you
are both the same with Lots of Love
and best wishes from Grandpa F. Horsfall

1456 Hamilton Ave St Louis Mo u.s.A.

Jan 20/36

Dear Ivy & Harry
just a few lines to thank you for
your lovely card and good wish
hope you will excuse me not writing
before as I have a voilent cold and
as I was writing Mom thought I
would make one job of it and give
uncle Sam value for stamps trusting
you are both well and heaps plenty
work with Lots of Love and Best
wishes for Both from
        Grandpa Fred Horsfall

1456 Hamilton Ave St Louis Mo
w. s. A.

March 12/36

Dear Ivy & Harry

recieved your welcome letter some
time ago; was sure glad to hear from
you: and to know that you were not
frurg to Death; but I dont think you have
such cold waves there as we do here; they
do everything sciantificaly here; they
have been testing out. this winter to
see how much frost it takes to kill a
person. if a person can stand 175 deg
rees below zero; they are Immune from
Frost Bite: it has been very low in
some parts of this country: but not so
low as that. I know it has been Durn
cold. thats swearing to it: but it is warming
up to-day but we have a fierce march
wind blowing; the Sun is getting more

powerful. I think they have lighted a few more fires in it; it feels like it anyway. I am very very sorry to inform you that mrs Hohman is moveing out of this Locality the later end of this month; she is going about a mile and half east and about a mile and half North. Now her husband has to take two cars to get to work; she is getting closer to his work so he dont have to Parkride it has been fierce this winter waiting at the Corners for Street Cars. Well; the Best thing I can do after she has gone is to go down on my knees and pray for somebody to come along with another Soup Bone. Nuff Sed; trusting this will find you Both fit and Raring to go. I am fairly well for a Kid shall be better I hope when the weather gets warmer with. Lots of Love and Best wishes from Grandpa

Fred Harshall

1456 Hamilton Ave St Louis mo u.s.a.

June 4/36

Dear Ivy & Harry

recieved your welcome letters some
time back; please excuse me not
answering before; as I have been very
busy with the garden after the hardest
winter I have put in here; my Climbing
Roses 8 — 9 — and 10 feet high I had to Cut
down to the ground all the Tops Killed
by severe frosts; I allways mulch
the roots every fall and that saved
them being Killed right out they
are growing again from the root
but it had taken me three years
to get them were I wanted them and
now another three to get them back.

Mom has been sending me some of those large Red; and yellow Gooseberry's seeds and I cannot get them to grow; for three years I have tried indoors and in the garden; nothing doing! perhaps Harry is aquainted with some won who grows them; who could Tell were I am wrong; they only grow those little green Tummy Ackes here I think I remember your Daily papers used to put in a Column on gardening you might try some in your own garden; anyway get Harry Interested he will find out. I was glad to hear you could grow Bitter sweet from seed I tried every which way; and could not get a shoot. Nuff Sed. only Lots of Love and Best wishes from Grandpa fred Horsfall

Epilogue

Some of the most extraordinary passages in this story are actually true facts, as are the following:

Ch 1, Frederick Thomas Horsfall was born in a tenement block in Wapping, East London. His father was a lighterman. Sarah was working as a sailmaker when she met Frederick.

Ch 2, Richard was a blacksmith's labourer. He and Jane did marry when she was seven months pregnant, twenty miles away, with no family present.

Ch 3, William was a ratcatcher. Wally did go with him that morning, and he was still telling the story when he was an old man. The Jennings family did keep bees, and William's mum was famed for her honey. John Jennings built Poplar House with its wonky roof; it still stands today and is still in the family.

Ch 4, The *Princess Alice* disaster did happen as described. Rivermen were paid to collect the floating bodies. Frederick did teach himself to read and write and then taught all his children.

Ch 6, Richard did take his family from Aston to London and onto Brisbane, Australia on the SS *Waroonga* and sadly died six months after arriving. His sons married and founded the dynasty Richard dreamed of. The name Spires was inadvertently changed to Spiers sometime during the emigration paperwork.

Ch 7, Florence did pack up school, aged eleven, to look after her family when her mother died. Frederick did read to his children every night.

Ch 8, Ernest did lose his pocket watch and was sent back by his father to find it. He did arrest the post office robber who was tried at the Old Bailey. Annie's sister Elizabeth was born deaf. She lived with her sister for nearly fifty years.

Ch 9, Arthur did sail to and then return from Australia. We don't know if he really met Florrie before he went, but I like to think that is why he returned.

Ch 10, Annie Jennings was really given a gold ring with diamonds for helping out a struggling family while the husband was away. Ernest never did find out. My mother was given the ring by Annie, along with its history, sixty years ago. She passed the legacy on to her granddaughter Courtney Spiers on her twenty-first birthday with the amazing story.

Ch 11, Harry did meet Christine Boyd in New York and go 'absent without leave' from the Royal Navy. He did take his tools around Missouri on a Harley Davidson while he was a Buick mechanic. Frederick Thomas Horsfall did leave a wife and two daughters in London to emigrate to St. Louis fifteen years after he sent two daughters from his first marriage there when they were only twelve and fifteen years old, respectively.

Ch 12, Arthur's first memory was seeing red-tunicked soldiers boarding ships to the Boer War. Arthur did collect the water every morning, and he did find his sister dead. Queenie did move into his street temporarily (fortunately for us, or this story may never have happened) while her father, Ernest, was waiting for a transfer to Brentford.

Ch 13, Fred Thomas Horsfall did travel all over the Pacific at the end of the nineteenth century, and his journal does still exist along with the powder pouch he was wearing when he was killed. He did bring home four Petrocelli paintings from Malta; I now have them. He was engaged to a Maltese girl when he was killed in the Battle of Jutland. We have pictures of her but no record of her real name. Family folklore said she never replied when told of his death.

Ch 14, Germany did temporarily halt the manufacture of sausages in order to build Zeppelins. Arthur did enlist and was invalided out of the King's Rifles before his eighteenth birthday. He did join the AVC (later the RAVC), and he was posted to France on the Western Front in 1916. His service record was lost, along with most of the RAVC records from the Great War in a bombing raid during the Second World War, so we do not know exactly where in France. He did send home drawings and silk postcards from the front, which I proudly keep safe. During his service, he narrowly escaped serious injury in a gas attack. Like many men from that war, Arthur very rarely spoke about his traumatic experiences.

Ch 15, The family always said they did not recognise Arthur when he first came home. He would probably have been diagnosed with post-traumatic stress disorder nowadays. Arthur was a fan of Marie Lloyd and did draw a geisha girl for Queenie. Arthur William Spiers did drink himself to death. There is a Jennings family legacy that a fortune is still in probate that nobody has managed to prove inheritance of; Ernest tried all his life. Arthur never did like Ernest, his father-in-law; they rarely met outside family occasions during the next fifty years. Ernest did try to convince Arthur to join the police, which he refused. Arthur was a bus conductor for twenty-four years. They did use their bus to take Arthur's mum home from shopping and smashed all the gas lamps in the street with the rocking of the bus. Arthur told the Aldgate joke until the day he died and still laughed at it every time. Queenie did have a silk wedding dress with an orange blossom wreath and a pink carnation bouquet.

Ch 16, Ernest did return to Poplar House, Great Bentley for his retirement. He bought out his brother and sister's shares in the cottage. Elizabeth Jessie Flewin did go there to live with Ernest and her sister Annie.

Ch.17, Florence did meet George Howell on the Woolwich ferry; he melted her heart with hot chocolate on the chilly winter mornings. Fred Spiers was stood up at the aisle. Doll did leave the factory because people there swore, and she did not like it.

Ch 18, Fred bought Wolsey Ave in 1929 with a mortgage from the United Juvenile Order for Total Abstinent Sons of the Phoenix. He did build a glass lean-to on the back. Ivy did have her wedding reception at no.72 Wolsey Avenue on a Tuesday, which Fred refused to attend as he did every other family wedding for the rest of his life.

Ch 19, Rose did miss her own funeral in St. Louis due to flooding. Ivy did send wedding cake all the way to America for her grandpa and her uncle. Grandpa Frederick never met Harry White, Ivy's new husband, but from his letters, seemed to have a genuine fondness for him. The letters are, of course, real and tell something of the hardships faced in depression-hit America in the 1930s. Also, of his love of gardening. Frederick is buried in St. Peters cemetery in St. Louis.

Frederick Thomas Horsfall signed off each letter the same, Nuff Sed.

About the Author

Glyn Spiers was born in Hornsey in North London; he now lives in Hertford. He has been married for over forty years and has managed his own engineering company since 1986. This is his first book.

Milton Keynes UK
Ingram Content Group UK Ltd.
UKHW020034121223
434176UK00001B/21